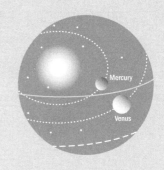

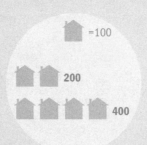

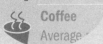

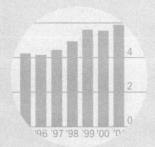

THE WALL STREET JOURNAL.
Guide to Information Graphics

THE WALL STREET JOURNAL.
Guide to Information Graphics

THE DOS AND DON'TS OF PRESENTING DATA, FACTS, AND FIGURES

Dona M. Wong

W. W. Norton & Company
New York | London

For information about permission to reproduce selections from this book, write to
Permissions, W. W. Norton & Company, Inc., 500 Fifth Avenue, New York, NY 10110

For information about special discounts for bulk purchases, please contact W. W. Norton
Special Sales at specialsales@wwnorton.com or 800-233-4830

Manufacturing by Courier Westford
Production manager: Anna Oler

Library of Congress Cataloging-in-Publication Data

Wong, Dona M.
The Wall Street Journal guide to information graphics : the dos and don'ts of presenting
data, facts, and figures / Dona M. Wong. — 1st ed.
       p. cm.
Includes indexes.
ISBN 978-0-393-07295-2 (hbk.)
1. Business presentations—Graphic methods. 2. Charts, diagrams, etc. 3. Visual
communication. I. Wall Street Journal. II. Title. III. Title: Guide to information graphics.
IV. Title: Dos and don'ts of presenting data, facts, and figures.
HF5718.22.W65 2010
658.4'52—dc22
                              2009035687

W. W. Norton & Company, Inc.
500 Fifth Avenue, New York, N.Y. 10110
www.wwnorton.com

W. W. Norton & Company Ltd.
Castle House, 75/76 Wells Street, London W1T 3QT

1 2 3 4 5 6 7 8 9 0

for my
parents

for my
better half
Joe

for Joyce &
Michael

Contents

Note: The charts in this book were generated with Excel, Deltagraph and Adobe Illustrator. However, there are many software packages available in the market and some are even freeware.

Introduction

We live in a data-driven world where the ability to create effective charts and graphs has become almost as indispensable as good writing.

With computer technology, anyone can create graphics, but few of us know how to do it well. Too often we present a chart with visual tricks such as clashing colors or 3-D blocks thinking it will look pretty, while not paying enough attention to conveying information.

Ultimately, it is content that makes graphics interesting. When a chart is presented properly, information just flows to the viewer in the clearest and most efficient way. There are no extra layers of colors, no enhancements to distract us from the clarity of the information.

Let's start with the three essential elements of good information graphics:

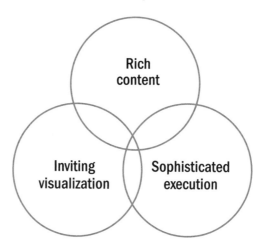

Rich content brings meaning to a graphic.

Inviting visualization interprets the content and highlights the essence of the information for the reader.

Sophisticated execution brings the content and the graphics to life.

Examples of confusing, misleading, and ineffective graphics are everywhere today. Many charts have sophisticated and intelligent underlying information, but the presentation fails to convey the intended message.

This book will have you saying "yikes" the next time you look at charts like the ones on the facing page because you will understand why they fall short.

These charts below may look okay to you, but they violate the basic principles of good charting. By the time you finish this book, you will be able to figure out why. If you must know now, you'll find the reasons why these charts do not work on page 143.

on page 143.

Examples of bad charting practices:

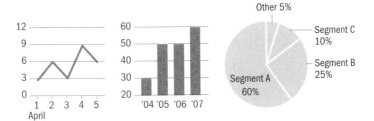

Unlike, say, language arts, the subject of information graphics is rarely taught in schools, nor is it part of on-the-job training. This leaves professionals in every industry scrambling to express themselves graphically.

My goal is to give you the critical foundation for assessing good and bad charts. By the end of the book, you will be able to express yourself in the language of graphics eloquently and effectively. I hope this book will find a permanent place on your desk.

THE WALL STREET JOURNAL.
Guide to Information Graphics

Typography
Legibility

Data

0.5

1.2

1.4

1.8

2.1

CHAPTER 1

The Basics

What really makes a chart effective are font, color and design and the depth of critical analysis displayed. In other words, do you have information worth making a chart for and have you portrayed it accurately? Remember that a single wrong data point can discredit the rest of the information and make the entire chart worthless.

In this chapter I provide practical guidelines and templates for fonts and the choice of colors — bright or muted. I answer questions like: Do two numbers constitute a chart? What is good data?

These basics provide the backbone and foundation for executing intelligent and persuasive charts.

How to create effective charts

The best charting practice is to systematically follow four essential steps — research, edit, plot and review.

Research

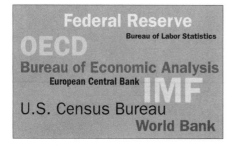

■ Research from up-to-the-minute authoritative sources.

■ Use an independent source for disputable data that is open to interpretation, such as market share, to avoid bias and conflict of interest.

■ Obtain permission to use the data, if required.

Edit

Absolute values		Percentage change	
A	B	A	B
10	100		
20	110	+100%	+10%
30	120	+200%	+20%

■ Identify your key message.

■ Choose the best data series to illustrate your point, e.g. market share vs. total revenue.

■ Filter and simplify the data to deliver the essence of the data to your intended audience.

■ Make numerical adjustments to the raw data to enhance your point, e.g. absolute values vs. percentage change.

3 Plot

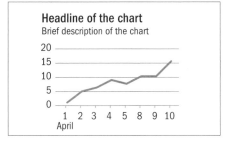

Headline of the chart
Brief description of the chart

■ Choose the right chart type to present the data, e.g. a line to show trend or a bar to show discrete quantities.

■ Choose the appropriate chart settings, e.g. scale, y-axis increments and baseline.

■ Label the chart, e.g. title, description, legends and source line.

■ Use color and typography to accentuate the key message.

4 Review

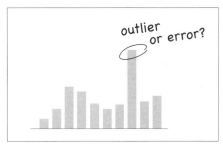

■ Check the plotted data against your sources.

■ Use judgment to evaluate whether your chart makes sense.

■ Try to look at the chart from the reader's perspective.

■ Verify your data with additional sources and consult with experts in the field for questionable content and outliers.

■ Refer to this book to check best charting practices.

Too often, this step is skipped for the sake of expedience. However, taking the time to go over every step of your work can make the difference between a professional and an amateur attempt. Unlike a misspelled word in a story, one wrong number discredits the whole chart.

Tangible evidence

When calculating the figures and plotting the graphs, use decimal places for accuracy. However, in labeling your chart, round off the numbers to the significant digit (or digits) for easy comparison. For example, labeling 12.345 may be more precise than 12.3, but it distracts from the visual impact of the chart.

Words vs. Charts

Charting is a powerful tool that puts a series of numbers in close proximity to each other. The numbers in a chart convey information to the reader both visually and narratively. The same set of numbers looks more concrete and precise when charted than when presented in a story or a caption.

Test

Numbers in a story:

Company A earns $100 million and outperforms company B which earns $75 million.

Numbers plotted:

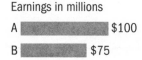

The chart shown above on the right allows you to make a judgment at a glance. It is more memorable than a string of numbers held together by words.

Let the data speak for itself

The best chart should be free of any distraction and allow the reader to compare or contrast the data and draw a conclusion.

A chart with obtrusions such as heavy gridlines and 3-D rendering obscures the data and diverts the reader's attention from the content.

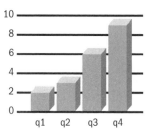

In contrast, a clean and crisp chart allows the reader to focus on the data, which is the message of the story.

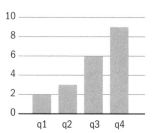

Create the right comparison

Same numbers, different stories

Filter and edit the data to keep it consistent and relevant to your message. Embellishments are not a substitute for organizing and presenting the data in the right way.

Example
Credit card issued by bank X in each country

Country	Number of credit cards	Population	Number of credit cards per capita
A	100 million	200 million	0.5
B	300	200	1.5
C	400	400	1.0

Presenting the number of credit cards on an aggregate basis and on a per capita basis will tell two different stories and convey different impressions with the same data.

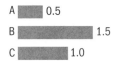

Number of credit cards, in millions

A ▮ 100
B ▮▮▮ 300
C ▮▮▮▮ 400

Number of credit cards per capita

A ▮ 0.5
B ▮▮▮ 1.5
C ▮▮ 1.0

Country C has the largest total market. This chart reflects the overall credit card market.

Country B has the highest issuance per capita. This chart demonstrates the success of the marketing effort in country B despite its smaller population.

If the raw data is insufficient to tell the story, do not add decorative elements. Instead, research additional sources and adjust data to stay on point.

Frame the reference

It's all relative
Imagine your wealthy uncle gave you $10,000. You would be happy. If you found out he had given your brother $20,000, would you still *feel* $10,000 richer? or $10,000 poorer?

$10,000 richer?

0   10,000

$10,000 poorer?

0   10,000   20,000

The frame of the information dictates how readers interpret the data. People need a reference point. **When you supply the reference point, you control the message.**

Readers frame the information based on what they expect to see. Even with a random number, they will create a reference point and assign meaning to it.

Quiz

Stock A is $100 a share.   A. ○ high
The share price is...   B. ○ low
                                C. ○ not sure

It is impossible to assess whether $100 is a fair price without any context. If we knew, for example, the 52-week high and low of stock A, we could answer this question.

Creating reference with charts
A single number by itself may not mean much. Plotting a series of numbers together can create an impact.

Example
A statement with a single number has no implication.

> Stock B is at $5 a share.

However, by plotting prices of stock B over time, the chart clearly shows that at $5, the stock has lost half its value.

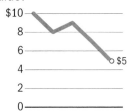

Send the right signal

One set of numbers can be charted in many ways. **People feel the pain of a $1,000 loss more than the joy of a $1,000 gain.** Use the right context to communicate the message you intend.

Example
Performance of stock A

Share price	Percent change from first data point
$ 8	0%
10	+25
8	0
4	-50
2	-75

Plotting the actual share prices:

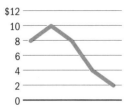

Plotting the percentage change in prices will bring the line into negative territory. This accentuates the drop in share prices. Just by setting the baseline, the chart visually implies the performance is unacceptable.

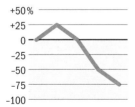

Both charts give a fair picture. Clearly, the choices you make in charting create the framework that sends a specific message to the readers.

The message of the chart should be consistent with ALL the facts and evidence available. For instance, when plotting profit and loss, a chart that omits previous quarters with poor performance would misrepresent the facts.

Example
Full disclosure

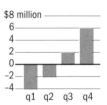

Half truth

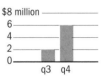

Tell the whole truth

Predicting the future?

Charting estimates with a definitive range or plotting projections far into the future gives a faulty impression of precision. Both practices use a precise tool to define arbitrary numbers.

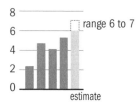

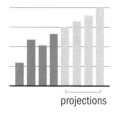

Do sweat the small stuff

Data is only as good as its source. Getting data from reputable and impartial sources is critical. For example, market share data should be benchmarked against a third party to avoid bias and add credibility.

Always assess data with a critical eye. If there is something wrong with one number, it is important to get to the bottom of it. One wrong data point can destroy the credibility of the whole chart.

Bad data + Good visualization = Bad chart

One size doesn't fit all

Every set of data requires individual analysis and interpretation. There are many ways to present and visualize the same set of data. The choice ultimately depends on the intended message.

Example
A bar chart shows the revenue of all the companies in a particular market.

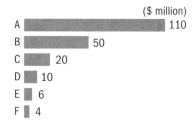

A pie chart, on the other hand, shows company A has 55% of the total market.

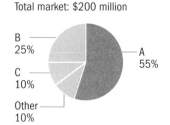

Put numbers in context

Build credibility by presenting facts fairly. An initiative to hire 200 people can be 1% of the workforce in one company or 10% in another company.

Showing a percentage without a base number is also meaningless. A 10% increase from what number to what number?

Example

Market share for product x

U.S.   Canada

A   B
60%   60%

The only conclusion we can draw from the two pie charts is that A and B both have a 60% market share. However, not knowing the size of each market makes it impossible to judge which has more sales.

Leave rounding to the end

Don't round off your numbers until the last step in the presentation process. Rounding the figures up and down during the analysis stage can lead to final results that are far from the truth and subsequent erroneous interpretations.

Example

	Data	After rounding
12.4		12
16.5		17
Percent change	+33.1%	+41.7%

Example

	Data	After rounding
Company A	$2.9 billion	$3 billion
Company B	3.1	3
Company C	4.2	4

The comparison between company A and B is lost. Besides, $0.2 billion or $200 million is a lot of money.

Beware of showing a big percentage change based on small numbers. It is generally unfair to compare the percentage change in revenue of a big company to that of a small company. Even if a small company increases its revenue threefold, it may still be a small sliver in the total market.

The more, the merrier?

Rich data means quality data — accurate data from reputable sources plus effective filtering of the data for the audience. In presentation, sometimes less is more.

Exercise judgment, edit

In the research stage, a bigger data set allows more in-depth analysis. In the edit phase, it is important to assess whether all your extra information buries the main point of the story or enhances the story and makes it more convincing.

Example

Without the benefit of editing and filtering, the bar charts show extensive detail of the revenues of all the companies in the market. However, the highlight of the story — the growth in market share of company B — is buried in the details.

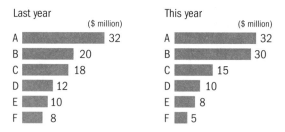

After analyzing the data, the pie charts show company B has a stronger market presence. Even though some details are lost in combining the smaller companies, the readers benefit from the editor's effort in highlighting the underlying data.

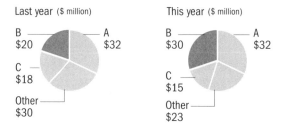

Tell the whole story with an excerpt
It is acceptable to extract a few numbers out of a series if these data points tell a story without misleading the reader to make wrong assumptions of the past and future.

Example
It is not deceiving to extract the recent performance data since sales have been basically rising at a steady rate. However, it is more advantageous to show all eight quarters to accentuate the point that performance has been consistently strong.

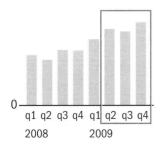

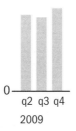

However, it would be misleading to extract the last three quarters in the chart below. In this case, excluding the previous quarters hides the bad performance data. The reader would draw a different conclusion if all the facts were shown.

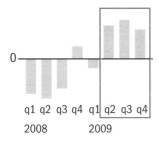

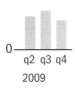

Data quantity does not equal data richness. Plotting a lot of data points is not necessarily better. A series of data points is meaningful and significant if it indicates a change from the baseline pattern.

Inconclusive

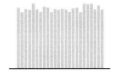

An upward trend

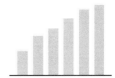

Legibility

With thousands of typefaces available today, in different styles and weights — serif, sanserif, italic, all caps, light, medium, bold and black — choosing type can be a daunting task. In the end, though, type in charts is meant to describe the information and not to adorn. And it is with that perspective that typography should be chosen purely on the merit of legibility.

Terminology

Serif type has a stroke added to the beginning or end of the main strokes of the letter.

Sanserif type means "letter without serifs."

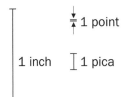

Type size is the height of the type, which originated from the height of the metal block on which the letter was cast. In digital type, the type size is the height of the assumed equivalent of the block, and not the dimension of the letter itself.

A point is the unit of measure for type size. Twelve points make a pica. A pica is close to one-sixth of an inch.

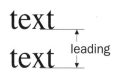

Leading *(pronounced led-ing)* is the vertical distance from the baseline of one line to the baseline of the next.

Basic rules of type legibility in charts

▨ In general, the leading should be about two points larger than the type size for comfortable reading, for example, 10-point type with 12-point leading.

▨ Don't set type too small or too condensed (condensed).

▨ Whether it is serif or sanserif, keep the type style simple. Use **bold** or *italic* only to emphasize a point. Don't use ***bold and italic*** at the same time.

▨ Don't use ALL CAPS. It is hard to read. Just like handwriting, we use upper- and lowercase letters.

▨ Avoid knocking white type out of black or color.

▨ Avoid hyphenation.

▨ Don't use highly stylized fonts (*stylized*).

▨ Don't set type at an angle.

▨ Don't track the type (t h i s   i s   t r a c k i n g).

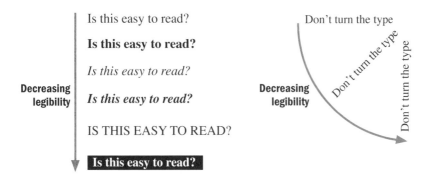

Simple test for legibility Reduce the chart on a copy machine to a reasonably small size. When typography is done right, the type will still be legible.

Typography in charts

In charts, typography should not be center stage. The data is the focus. Type in charts is there to describe the chart clearly and not to evoke an emotion, as in a fashion magazine or political poster. Poor typography draws undue attention away from the underlying data, which carries the main message. The impulse to use type styles to spice up the chart should be avoided at all costs. Typography done right helps present the information in the most efficient and direct way.

 Don't permit typography to oppress the underlying data.

 Keep the typography simple. The headline can be either bold or a couple of sizes larger.

Don't use all caps or knock white type → out of black.

Don't use → bold italic.

Don't use bold for the → numbers on the scale.

Don't set type at an → angle.

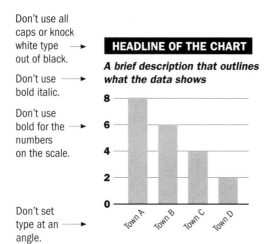

HEADLINE OF THE CHART

A brief description that outlines what the data shows

Headline of the chart

A brief description that outlines what the data shows

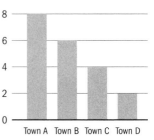

Town A   Town B   Town C   Town D

Alternatively, chart the data as horizontal bars to accommodate long names.

Town A ... 8
Town B ... 6
Town C ... 4
Town D ... 2

Don't use highly stylized fonts or turn the type sideways to save space.

ℌeadline of the chart

A brief description that outlines what the data shows

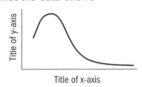

 Serif and sanserif fonts can complement each other and add variety, and are still highly legible.

Headline of the chart

A brief description that outlines what the data shows

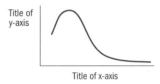

 Don't knock white type out of black or color. Legibility is compromised.

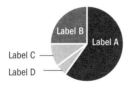

 Use bold to increase legibility on a shaded background or to emphasize a segment.

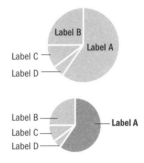

 Don't set a huge amount of text in bold. Emphasizing everything means nothing gets emphasized.

Name	Data	Data	Data
Company A	0.0	**0.0**	**0.0**
Company B	0.0	**0.0**	**0.0**
Company C	0.0	**0.0**	**0.0**
Company D	0.0	**0.0**	**0.0**

 Use bold type to emphasize the focal point of the message. Be judicious.

Name	Data	Data	Data
Company A	0.0	0.0	**0.0**
Company B	0.0	0.0	**0.0**
Company C	0.0	0.0	**0.0**
Company D	0.0	0.0	**0.0**

Rich data, high visual impact

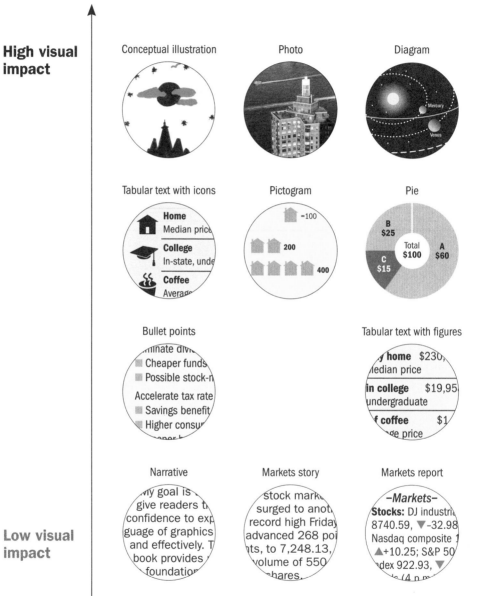

High visual impact

Conceptual illustration

Photo

Diagram

Mercury

Venus

Tabular text with icons

Home
Median price

College
In-state, unde

Coffee
Averag

Pictogram

=100

200

400

Pie

B
$25

C
$15

Total
$100

A
$60

Bullet points

minate divi
Cheaper funds
Possible stock-n
Accelerate tax rate
Savings benefit
Higher consu

Tabular text with figures

y **home** $230
ledian price

in **college** $19,95
undergraduate

f **coffee** $1
ge price

Narrative

 My goal is
give readers t
confidence to ex
guage of graphics
and effectively. T
book provides
foundatio

Markets story

stock mark
surged to anot
record high Friday
advanced 268 poi
nts, to 7,248.13,
volume of 550
shares.

Markets report

–Markets–
Stocks: DJ industri
8740.59, ▼–32.98
Nasdaq composite
▲+10.25; S&P 50
dex 922.93, ▼

Low visual impact

Sparse data

34

Chart with photo

Map

Albany Street

Rector Place

West Street

RECTOR PARK

West Thames Street

Data map

1
2
3

Display package with multiple charts and photos

me of Package
scription of charts

April   May

Vertical bars

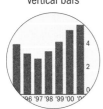

4

2

0

'96 '97 '98 '99 '00 '0

Line

10

9

8

F M A M J

Multiple charts

28%
26
20
19
6

Charts and tables

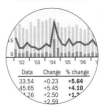

.5

0

'02 '03 '04 '05 '06 '0

Data	Change	% change
33.54	+0.23	**+5.64**
45.65	+5.45	**+4.10**
.26	+2.50	**+1.2**
	+2.59	

Horizontal bars

A	7.7
y B	6.4
ny C	4.2
y D	2.1
	1.8

Graphs within a table

ange	% change
+0.23	**+5.64**
+5.45	**+4.10**
+2.50	**+1.24**
+2.59	**+0.1**
28	**–1**

Table of numbers

Data	Change	% c
33.54	+0.23	**+5.64**
45.65	+5.45	**+4.10**
34.26	+2.50	**+1.24**
23.52	+2.59	**+0.1**
2.11	–1.28	**–1**
	–0.97	

Stock listing

	52-week		
Sym)	High	Low	Clo
idic AA	52.25	42.15	45.1
ro AB	12.13	10.17	11.17
hip AC	8.36	4.26	6.26
ta AD	66.46	51.02	55.02
en AE	28.08	21.12	25.12
AF	4.36	2.26	3.0
AG	9.46	6.02	
	44.08	39.1	

Rich data

Conceptual illustration by Joyce Koltisko; photo composition for chart with photo by Michael Koltisko

Color

Basics

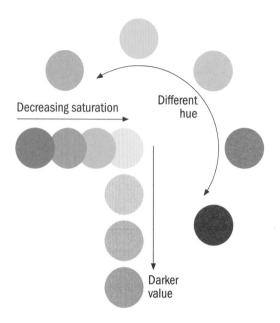

Decreasing saturation

Different hue

Darker value

Describing colors

There are three main attributes of a color: hue, saturation and value.

Hue is how we normally describe color such as red, green and blue.

Saturation is the intensity of the color. A color with higher saturation is more intense in the same hue. For instance, a red becomes a more intense red (less pinkish) as the saturation increases.

Value is how light or dark a color is. A darker shade of a color can be achieved by adding black ink.

Warm and cool colors

Warm colors are those in the red area of the color spectrum such as red, orange, yellow and brown. Cool colors are the blue side of the spectrum and include blue, green and neutral gray.

Warm colors appear larger than cool colors so red can visually overpower blue even if used in equal amounts. Warm colors appear closer while cool colors visually recede.

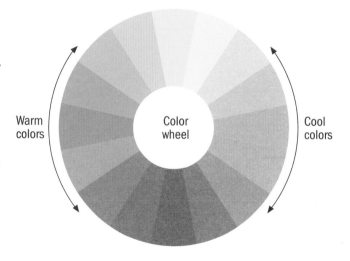

Warm colors

Color wheel

Cool colors

Specifying colors

Colors can be specified in different ways, depending on the application.

CMYK

Cyan, magenta, yellow, black are the four inks used by printers to produce full-color printing. In theory, overprinting cyan, magenta and yellow produces black, but in reality, the combination is a muddy brown. Black is used as the fourth printing ink to get a crisp solid black. Colors are specified as percentages of these inks.

Example
CMYK (100, 30, 0, 0) will print a color with 100% cyan, 30% magenta, 0% yellow and 0% black.

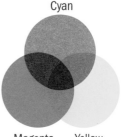

Cyan

Magenta   Yellow

RGB

Red, green and blue light sources are combined to display colors on television and computer monitors. When all three lights illuminate simultaneously, white light is produced. When working with images for the screen, colors are assigned by the amount of red, green and blue. The range of each color component runs from 0 to the highest value 255.

Example
Red   RGB (255, 0, 0)

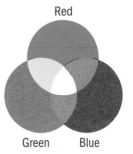

Red

Green   Blue

Hex value/hex triplet

A six-digit hexadecimal number or triplet is used to define colors in web design. Colors can be specified in the format of #RRGGBB, where RR, GG, and BB are the hexadecimal values for the red, green and blue values of the color. The range of each color component is from #00 to the highest value #FF.

Example
Red   RGB (255,0,0)   #FF0000
Green   RGB (0,255,0)   #00FF00
Blue   RGB (0,0,255)   #0000FF

Color palettes

A color palette for charts should include the basic colors and three to five shades of each hue. This gives you the option of using fewer colors within a chart to avoid distraction. Once you choose a palette, stay with it for the entire presentation so all the visuals look coordinated.

Bright color palette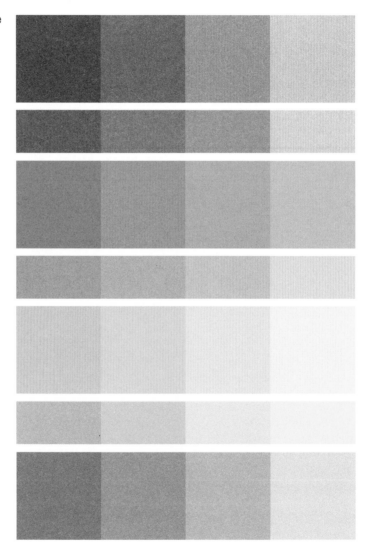

Muted color palette

Color in charts

Admit colors into charts gracefully, as you would receive in-laws into your home. Don't apply all the colors in your palette at the same time. Using too many colors in a single chart is confusing and garish. Instead, choose harmonious combinations, such as different shades of the same color or colors on the same side of the color wheel. Limit the scope — even if color is available, it is okay not to use it at all.

Don't choose your colors arbitrarily. Choose them strategically to compare and contrast your data effectively. Every time you change a color, it signifies a change in information or an added layer of data. Ultimately, the information you present should determine every color you choose for your charts.

 Don't use multiple colors to represent the same kind of data.

 Use the same color to represent the same variable so the readers can focus on comparing the data.

A darker shade or a different color can be used to highlight the focal point.

 Don't use different colors or colors on the opposite side of the color wheel in a multiple-bar chart. The color contrast distracts the reader from the data.

 Use graduating shades of one color or colors on the same side of the color wheel to keep a multiple-bar chart clean and crisp. The readers can then focus on the underlying data.

Don't set the scale with alternating light and dark colors in the middle of the scale. The eyes can't draw meaningful comparison jumping between light and dark shades.

 The color scale should graduate from lightest to darkest or vice versa, regardless of the color. A simple test is to convert the color scale to black and white and check for smooth progression from light to dark.

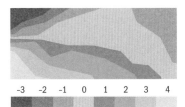

-3 -2 -1 0 1 2 3 4

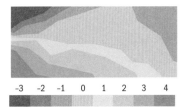

-3 -2 -1 0 1 2 3 4

Test: Convert the color scale to gray scale to test for the gradation.

Abrupt jump from
lightest to darkest shade

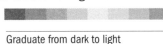

Graduate from dark to light
and on to dark

 In general, avoid thematic representation of colors, such as red and green to show Christmas sales.

 Colors can reflect the tone, for instance, deep blue for conservative and bright colors for something cheerful.

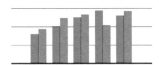

 Don't use red for positive numbers in a bar chart. Red is strongly associated with losses in business.

 Depicting negative earnings in red bars can be highly effective.

Color chart templates

With the bright color palette

Use different shades of the same color or colors on the same side of the color wheel.

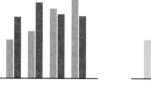
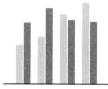
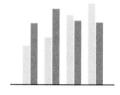

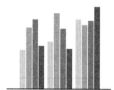
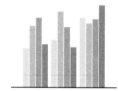
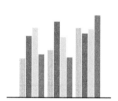

Use bright or dark colors such as red and black to emphasize the important line.

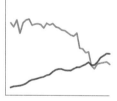
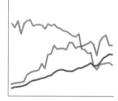

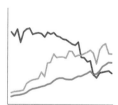
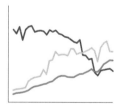

Use a darker shade or a different color to highlight a segment.

With the muted color palette

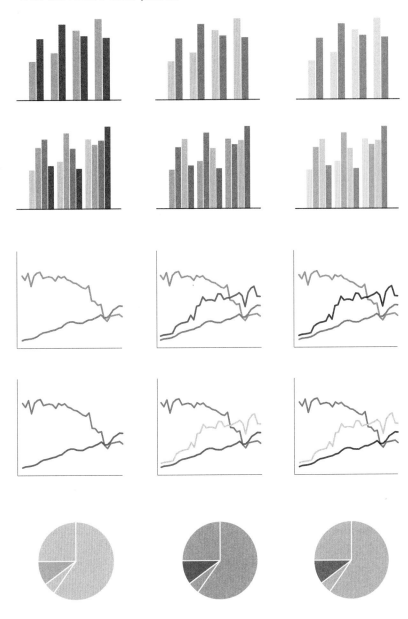

Coloring for the color blind

A color change in any chart element signifies a change in information or an added layer of data. If color is a carrier of information and is not seen, the translation of information is severely impeded. A chart is only successful if a reader can access, read and understand the content.

According to the National Institutes of Health, about 1 in 10 men have some form of color blindness. There are two major types of color blindness. The most common form is distinguishing between red and green and the other type is distinguishing between blue and yellow.

Color combination pitfalls

Color combinations such as red/green or blue/yellow are on opposite sides of the color wheel. The color hues are very different but they can be similar in value or lightness. The color intensity overpowers the underlying data. The colors even vibrate when used in large quantities. These color combinations are distracting for readers with normal color vision. The lack of contrast in lightness makes it virtually unreadable for color-blind users.

A legend that relies on color alone to convey information can be extra work for general users and possibly indecipherable for color-blind readers. Legends are often difficult for most readers since our eyes cannot draw immediate distinction between small color swatches, especially when there is not enough contrast in color and value.

Different hues, same value

Color text and legends

Company A
Company B

Product x
Product y

Lack of contrast when converted to black and white:

Company A
Company B

Product x
Product y

Strategies for selecting effective colors

1 Set type in black

Black provides the highest contrast. It is most effective to use black type on a light background. Color type is hard to read even for readers with normal color vision. If you need a dark background for design reasons, use white type and not color type.

2 Label directly on chart elements

Direct labeling is helpful for all readers. If you must use a legend, be sure the colors have high contrast in values.

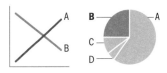

In addition to using darker shades to highlight a bar or a line, you can set the label in bold typeface. See segment B in the pie chart on the right. This redundant means of presenting information will guarantee all information conveyed with color is also clear without color.

3 Ensure high contrast in values

If a different color is used to distinguish different chart elements or signify a change in data, use a lighter or darker shade of that second color. It is easier for the eyes to differentiate lightness or darkness. Sufficient contrast in values makes the chart more accessible to all readers.

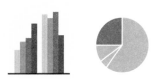

4 Final test: Convert to gray scale

Print the chart in black and white or make a copy in gray scale to test whether the contrast in values, not colors, is sufficient. The colors work if the chart holds up in black and white.

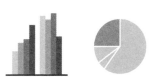

Color scale application

The **heat map** is one of the tools that investors use to identify new opportunities in changing markets so that they can then take advantage of them. Juxtaposing a series of heat maps can help reveal how prices of different securities move together.

Example
Change in volatility in a stock index option over the course of a trading day.

Strike price

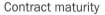

Contract maturity

Color is the third dimension that is used to show the relationship among three variables in a flat display. These heat maps show how the change in options volatility depends on both contract maturity and strike price over time.

Any measure that shows a continuous range of values can be mapped with a color gradient.

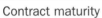

Change in volatility

(–)   0   +

Overall, the color scale should graduate smoothly from lightest to darkest or vice versa, regardless of the color. There should not be alternating dark and light strips in the middle of the spectrum.

CHAPTER 2

Chart Smart

Correct
Effective

Incorrect
Inadequate

When creating a chart, it is you who interprets the data and selects the format that most effectively presents complex information. The underlying principles that I lay out in this chapter, when applied judiciously, can take your chart from ordinary to powerful.

In this chapter, I specifically address good chart choices and bad chart choices. I have set up each topic in a two-page spread, with the bad charting practices on the left and the correct approach on the right. You will see that some choices are strictly right or wrong; others are either more effective or simply lack essential information. For example, imagine reading a pie chart as you would a clock. It makes the most sense to place the largest segment of the pie on the right at 12 o'clock. This emphasizes its importance.

Height and weight

Never shade below a line unless the chart has a zero baseline. Filling in below a line turns a line chart into an area graph. Just like a bar chart, an area graph measures discrete quantities. Coloring below a fever line that does not start at zero truncates data.

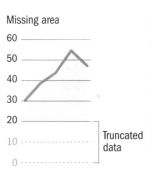

Missing area

60
50
40
30
20
10 ············· Truncated
0 ············· data

Misrepresenting the trend

The purpose of a line chart is to show a trend. Choosing a y-axis scale that yields a flat line totally defeats the purpose. On the other hand, an exaggerated line creates a drama that may not be a fair representation of the data.

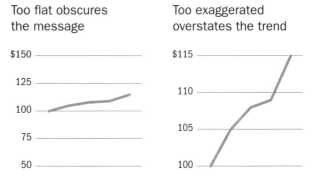

Too flat obscures   Too exaggerated
the message   overstates the trend

$150 $115

125   110

100

                            105
75

                            100
50

Missing the twists and turns

A line chart can show massive amounts of data in a very small space. A thin line could fade into the background. However, a thick line obscures the data points between peaks and troughs.

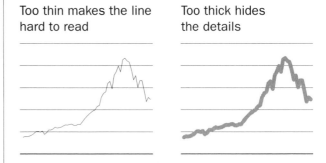

Too thin makes the line   Too thick hides
hard to read   the details

The right height — two-thirds of the chart area

Choose the y-axis scale so that the height of the fever line occupies roughly two-thirds of the chart area. The scale should also encompass relevant reference points, which help determine the range and make it less arbitrary. For example, the range of a stock chart should include its 52-week high and low.

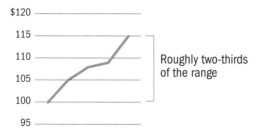

Roughly two-thirds of the range

The right weight — visible with details

The weight of the fever line should be thick enough to stand out against the grid line but still thin enough to show the twists and turns of the line. Keep the grid lines thin and the zero baseline slightly thicker than the rest of the grid lines.

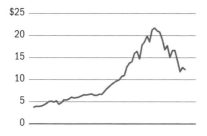

Lines are best used to display continuous data series over a period of time, such as stock prices and index values. Lines are suited for showing trend, acceleration or deceleration, and volatility, including sudden peaks or troughs.

Unlike a bar chart, a fever line doesn't necessarily require a zero baseline. For example, plotting a stock index with a range in the thousands from a zero baseline would make it hard to discern daily changes.

Terminology

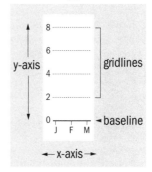

Lines

Y-axis increments

Even though a line chart does not have to include a zero baseline, avoid starting a y-axis with values that are close to zero. If adding a couple of grid lines can cover the zero baseline, do so.

Bad increments

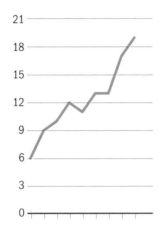

Bad baseline

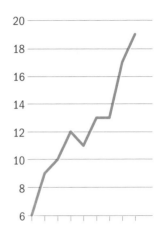

Awkward increments

- 0, 3, 6, 9, 12, 15
- 0, 4, 8, 12, 16, 20
- 0, 6, 12, 18, 24, 30
- 0, 8, 16, 24, 32, 40
- 0, 12, 24, 36, 48
- 0, 15, 30, 45, 60
- 0, 0.4, 0.8, 1.2, 1.6

While the chart above right uses acceptable y-axis increments — 6, 8, 10, 12, etc. — the fever line starts at the value "6," which makes the upward trend appear more dramatic than it actually is.

Two examples with good use of increments

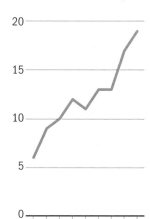

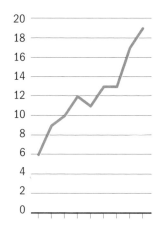

Keep it simple and **use the increments people naturally use when counting:** 0, 5, 10, 15, 20, etc. Readers can easily recognize a data point in between two grid lines.

Natural increments

▪ 0, 1, 2, 3, 4, 5

▪ 0, 2, 4, 6, 8, 10

▪ 0, 5, 10, 15, 20

▪ 0, 10, 20, 30, 40, 50

▪ 0, 25, 50, 75, 100

▪ 0, 0.2, 0.4, 0.6, 0.8, 1.0

▪ 0, 0.25, 0.50, 0.75, 1.00

Clean lines, clear signal

Even if color is available, do not plot more than four lines on a single chart. You won't find a pot of gold at the end of that rainbow.

No spaghetti lines

To differentiate each line, it is tempting to try out all the dashed lines and shape markers in the graphics software toolbox. But they only obscure the lines which carry the information.

You can use solid lines exclusively by limiting the chart to four or fewer lines. Varying weights and shades do the work of differentiating the lines more effectively than distracting patterns and markers.

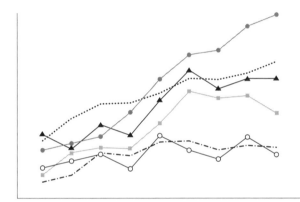

Four or fewer lines

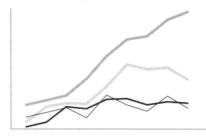

In a single chart, keep the maximum number of lines to three or possibly four if the lines are not intersecting at many points. Select the three or four data series that will convey a difference. More is not necesssarily better. The purpose of a multiple-line chart is to compare and contrast different data series. Plotting too many lines on the same chart gives a confusing picture and defeats the whole purpose.

Panel of charts

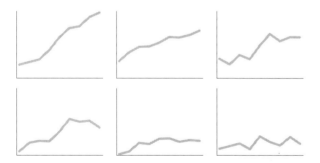

With four or more data series, an array of individual charts can display a pattern and allows better comparison among all the lines than a spaghetti chart. This way the clarity of each individual line is preserved.

In a black-and-white multiple-line chart, the darkest line should represent the most important data series. In a color chart, the most important line should be one color, for instance, red, and the other lines should be shades of a second color, such as blue. Using different colored lines could be confusing and may be illegible for color-blind readers.

Legends and labels

Do not label the line with a large block of text that overwhelms the line. Keep your label concise, no more than one short sentence.

Here, the text weighs down the line.

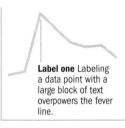

Label one Labeling a data point with a large block of text overpowers the fever line.

Avoid labeling at long distance

A legend separated from the line requires the readers to do extra work cross-referencing between the key and the line.

It is hard for readers to focus on the relationship between the lines while their eyes dart back and forth from the legend to the chart.

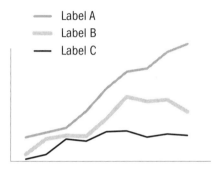

❶ Point one Description text goes in this space. Text goes in this space.

❷ Point two Description text goes in this space. Text goes in this space.

❸ Point three Description text goes in this space. Text goes in this space.

Label the lines directly

A legend need not be in a small box tucked into the corner of the chart. Direct labeling allows the reader to identify the lines quickly and focus on comparing and contrasting the patterns.

Use a legend only when space is tight and the lines intersect extensively. The order of the legend should match the ranking of the end points since they are the most current data points.

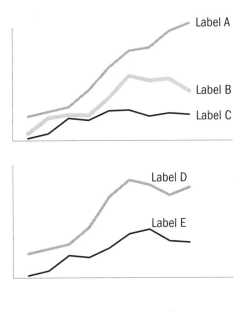

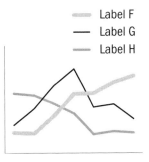

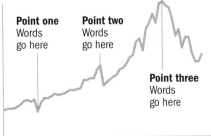

Left-right y-axis scales

Do not use left-right scales when the two data series measure the same kind of quantities, such as stock prices. Instead, use a comparable scale or chart the percentage changes to compare the two series.

Do not mix apples and oranges

Do not chart two uncorrelated series with one scale on the left and another one on the right. Saving space is not a good reason.

Example
Revenue is plotted against a market index on a double y-axis scale.

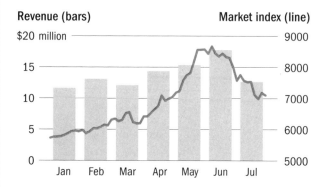

One can argue the stock market influences sales, but the relationship is not direct or measurable. Overlaying the two variables only makes your chart more confusing.

Moving in tandem

Using left-right y-axis scales can help show how two directly related series move together.

Example
The chart below shows how an increase in market share has not helped generate more revenue.

Revenue (bars) **Market share (line)**

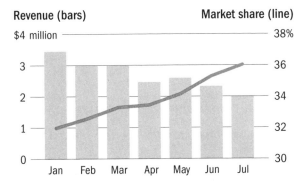

Always label the scales clearly to avoid any confusion.

Adhere to the correct chart type for each series — lines for continuous data and bars for discrete quantities. Do not deviate for stylistic reasons. The only exception is when both data series call for a chart with vertical bars. In such instances, convert one to a line.

Use left-right scales sparingly. Your choice of scale can change the apparent relationship between the two lines.

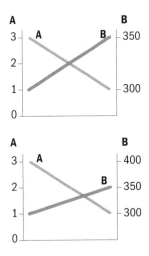

Comparable scales

Don't use awkward y-axis increments when calculating the ranges of the comparable scales.

Biased comparison

Anytime two or more charts are juxtaposed in the same space, the reader will compare and contrast the lines. Plotting the data series on noncomparable scales gives an unfair representation of the data.

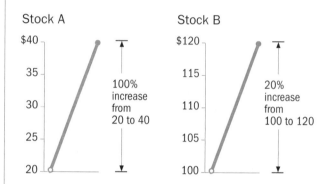

Both stock A and stock B increased by $20. Stock A doubled in value while stock B increased by 20% in the same period. Yet the pictures show that both lines have the same slope.

Unless the readers calculate the percentage changes of both lines, they will draw the wrong conclusion.

The charts above wrongly suggest that investors in stock A and stock B are getting the same return on their investments.

Fair comparison

When contrasting two or more sets of data, use comparable scales.

Relative performance should be obvious to the reader from the slopes of the lines. The ranges of the y-axis on both charts should represent the same percentage change.

When data series are in similar ranges, it is best to plot them on the same chart for easy and immediate comparison.

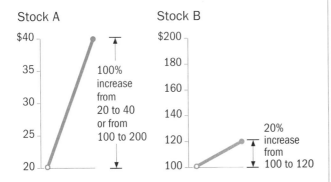

In this example, the range of the y-axis scale from $20 to $40 is the same percentage change as from $100 to $200.

Even though both stock A and stock B increased by $20, investors in stock A are five times better off than investors in stock B during that period.

Vertical Bars

Form and shading

Don't create shadows behind bars. A bar chart is not a piece of fine art. The shadow contains no information or data.

Bars too narrow

Vertical bars measure discrete quantities. When the bars are too narrow, your eyes focus on the negative space, the space between the bars, which carries no data.

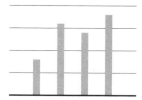

Distracting shades

Since all the bars measure the same variable, different shades have no relevance to the data. They only distract the readers from comparing the bars.

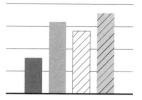

Where is the top of the bar?

Three-dimensional vertical bars are flat out wrong. The reader is left to guess where the top of the bar meets the grid. Rendering the bars in 3-D adds no information.

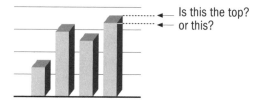

Is this the top? or this?

Let the bar stand on its own

The width of the bars should be about twice the width of the space between the bars.

All the bars in a single chart should be the same color and shade since they measure the same variable.

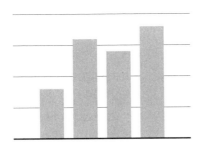

Projections and estimates

A lighter-shaded bar can be used to distinguish projections and estimates from actual values.

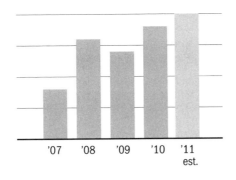

A gray background can be used to identify the negative zone of a bar chart.

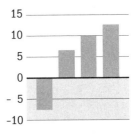

Zero baseline

Even if you make the bottoms of the bars jagged to signify that the chart doesn't start at a zero baseline, it is difficult to compare the total value of each bar.

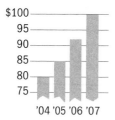

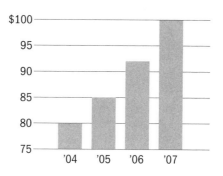

Truncation equals misrepresentation

A bar chart that doesn't begin at a zero baseline is misleading. **Truncation obscures the discrete total value of each bar** and makes comparison of the data difficult.

In the above example, the chart appears to show that revenue in 2007 was five times that of 2004 — while in reality, revenue in 2007 rose only 25% from 2004. But the only way a reader would know that is to calculate the figures — which defeats the purpose of the chart.

For better representation of the same data, see the charts on the facing page.

Start at the zero baseline — No exceptions!

Vertical bars are used to depict **discrete quantities**, particularly for measuring distinct sets of data, such as revenue and income, over a period of time.

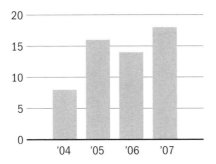

Draw the zero baseline thicker and heavier than the rest of the grid lines.

Always label the value of a vertical bar if it is close to zero.

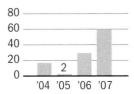

Alternative charting

If the data points are close in value and the bars are indistinguishable in height, it may be more effective to plot the point changes or percentage changes.

Year	Revenue	Change from a year ago
2004	$ 80 million	
2005	85	+$ 5 million
2006	92	+ 7
2007	100	+ 8

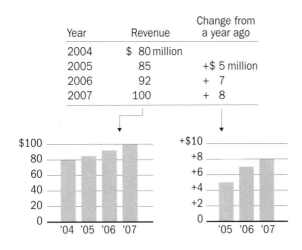

Multiple bars and legends

Don't label vertical bars with type at an angle on the x-axis. Instead, plot the data as horizontal bars.

Illegible text

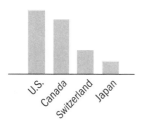

Alternative charting

No zebra pattern

Alternating light and dark bars make the reader dizzy. Comparison of the data is impossible.

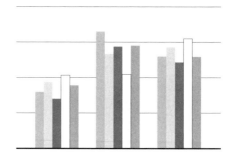

No backward legend

Listing the elements of a legend in a different order from the sequence of the bars is confusing.

A legend gives the readers the key to the information. It should not be positioned below the chart.

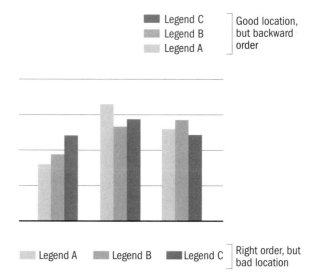

From lightest to darkest

The shading of the bars should move from lightest to darkest for easy comparison.

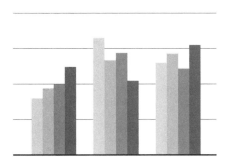

The right sequence

A legend can be used in a multiple-bar chart since labeling directly on a chart can be messy.

The order of the elements in a legend should be in the same sequence as the bars for easy reference. Why make your reader do extra work?

Two ways to display a legend:

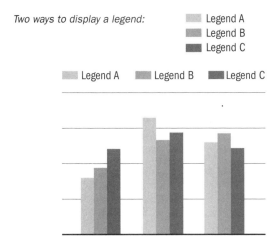

Keep multiple-bar charts to four or fewer categories. It is difficult for the reader to visually compare and contrast five or more bars. This principle applies even if color is available. Rainbow color bars are even more difficult to follow.

Direct labeling is practical with two categories in a multiple-bar chart. With three or four categories, a legend should be used for a cleaner presentation.

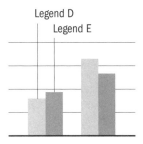

Broken bars and outliers

Don't shorten a broken bar to make it a similar height to the rest of the bars. An outlier should be well above all the other bars and still look like an outlier.

Data sample too small

Don't break a bar if the data series has fewer than a dozen data points. The data sample is too small to judge which data point is the outlier.

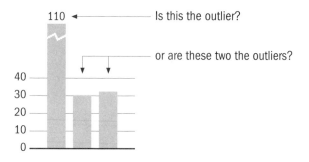

Values too close

Don't break a bar if its value is only about two times the next largest value. Just extend the scale and plot it as a regular bar.

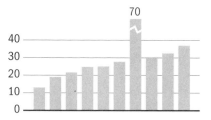

Use broken bars sparingly

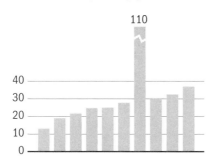

A broken bar may be used to display an outlier in a vertical bar chart. However, before you break a bar confirm that ...

☑ The data source provided the correct value for the outlier.

☑ There are at least ten bars and only one outlier.

☑ The outlier is about three times or more the size of the next largest value.

☑ The outlier is not the point of the story. For instance, last year's revenue was three times the normal level. A broken bar for that data point would diminish the visual impact of that exceptional performance.

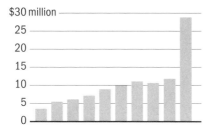

Choose a y-axis scale so that all the bars except the outlier are comfortably positioned in the chart.

Always label the data point of the broken bar.

Ordering and regrouping

Just as in a vertical bar chart, do not use different shades or 3-D rendering in a horizontal bar chart.

Similar to a vertical multiple-bar chart, a horizontal multiple-bar chart should be kept to four or fewer categories. The shading of the bars should be assigned from lightest to darkest so the reader can easily compare and contrast the data.

No random lineup

Don't plot horizontal bars in a random order. The main quality of a horizontal bar chart is the ranking of items by the same attribute. Plotting the bars in an arbitrary sequence defeats the purpose.

Avoid grid lines and scale

Horizontal bars are not as easy to compare as vertical bars. Using a scale and grid lines would make it even harder to discern the relative lengths of the bars. Direct labeling is cleaner and clearer.

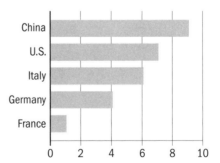

The right order

A horizontal bar chart is most useful when ranking the items by the same characteristic, such as ranking the countries by sales of a product.

The bars should be ranked from the largest to the smallest or vice versa. A specific bar can be highlighted with a different shade.

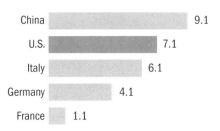

China	9.1
U.S.	7.1
Italy	6.1
Germany	4.1
France	1.1

The exception to the rule of ranking by value is when a specific order, such as alphabetical order, is necessary to facilitate easier reading. An example would be plotting a chart with 50 states.

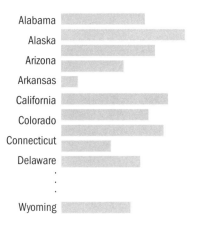

Alabama
Alaska
Arizona
Arkansas
California
Colorado
Connecticut
Delaware
.
.
.
Wyoming

When plotting horizontal bars over time, the bars should be ordered from the most recent data point and go back in time.

2010
2009
2008
2007
2006

For a long list of horizontal bars, label the data points flush right and use thin rules to separate the bars in groups of three to five to help the readers read across.

A	12.1
B	11.1
C	10.1
D	9.1
E	8.1
F	7.1
G	6.1
H	5.1
I	4.1
J	3.1
K	2.1
L	1.1

Negative bars

Avoid using horizontal bars if most of the values are negative. It is best to use vertical bars unless the labels do not fit underneath the bars. A picture with the bars below a horizontal baseline leaves a stronger impression than one with bars to the left of a zero line.

Negative values in a horizontal bar chart

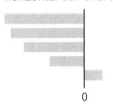

A more striking picture as a vertical bar chart

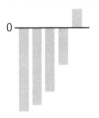

Wrong direction

Never plot horizontal bars with negative values on the right side of the zero line, even if there are no positive numbers in the data set.

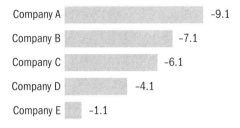

Company A	-9.1
Company B	-7.1
Company C	-6.1
Company D	-4.1
Company E	-1.1

No two-way horizontal bars

Demographics charts sometimes plot the number of males on one side and females on the other. However, in most applications, the left side of the baseline is reserved for negative numbers. It is hard to compare two sets of bars on opposite sides. It is better to plot the two data series as a multiple-bar chart.

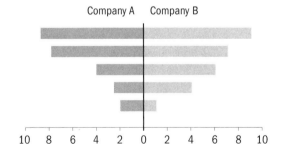

Company A   Company B

10 8 6 4 2 0 2 4 6 8 10

Left is negative, right is positive

Always keep the negative numbers on the left side of the zero line, even if the entire data set consists of negative values. The right side of the baseline is reserved for positive numbers only. A zero baseline can be added to reinforce the negative zone.

It is acceptable to shade the negative bars to further distinguish them from the positive bars.

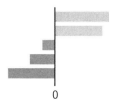

0

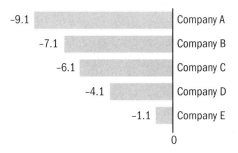

Align the labels on either side of the baseline or keep them all flush left.

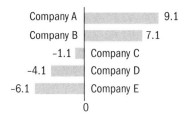

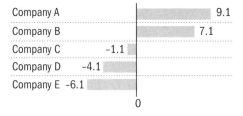

Slicing and dicing

Pie charts should not be used to illustrate complicated relationships among many segments. It is easier to compare two vertical bars than two slices in a pie.

Less effective order

It's intuitive to read top to bottom and clockwise. **Never chart segments clockwise from smallest to largest.** By ordering the slices from smallest to largest in clockwise direction or vice versa, the least important segment has the most prominent position.

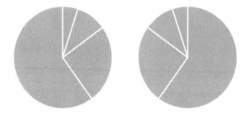

Too many slices

It's difficult to compare and contrast many segments. **A pie chart shouldn't have more than five slices.**

If there are more than five, combine the smaller and less significant segments to create the fifth slice and label it "Other." If all segments have to be represented separately, use a stacked or segmented bar chart instead. See page 79.

Larger segments on top

start here

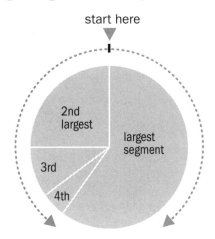

Reading a pie chart is like reading a clock. It's intuitive to start at 12 o'clock and go clockwise.

Therefore, it is most effective to **place the largest segment at 12 o'clock on the right to emphasize its importance.**

The best way to order the rest of the segments is to place the second biggest slice at 12 o'clock on the left; the rest would follow counterclockwise. The smallest slice will fall near the bottom of the chart, in the least significant position.

The only exception to the ordering is when all the slices are close in value. In this case, start at 12 o'clock on the right and go clockwise from largest to smallest.

Just like in bar and line charts, direct labeling helps the reader to quickly identify individual segments and focus on the comparison between them.

Dressing up the slices

Pie charts are not as effective in presenting complex data as line or bar charts, but they are good visual tools for showing portions of a whole. Avoid the temptation to dress up a pie by using different colors or 3-D effects, which will distort how the reader perceives the data. **Any embellishments that are not relevant to the data have no place in a chart.**

Distracting shades and colors

A pie with multiple shades or colors distracts the reader from immediate comparison of the segments.

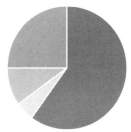

Special effect overkill

Don't use more than one trick to highlight a segment, for instance, don't both shade and pull out the slice you want to emphasize.

Incorrect data representation

Since the area is used to represent each segment's relative value, a pie with three-dimensional rendering misrepresents each segment's proportion to the whole.

Keep the shading simple

It is generally easier to compare different lengths than different sizes of segments of a pie. Therefore, keep it simple when shading the slices. The goal is for the reader to compare the size of any segment to the whole pie efficiently.

Highlight the important slice

Use different shading to highlight one or two important segments.

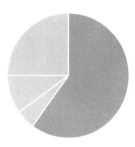

The highlighted segment doesn't have to be the largest slice. However, do not reorder the segments.

A donut pie chart can be used to display the total value inside the pie.

Slicing a slice

The function of charts is to give an immediate impression of a visual message. Asking readers to do the math in their heads totally defeats the purpose of charting. Always do the work for your readers.

Stop slicing already*!*

While pie charts are commonly used in the business world, it is not always the ideal format in which to compare and contrast different segments visually. Therefore, **segmenting within a slice makes the second segment difficult to grasp.** It's too much work for most readers to compare the final slice to the original pie.

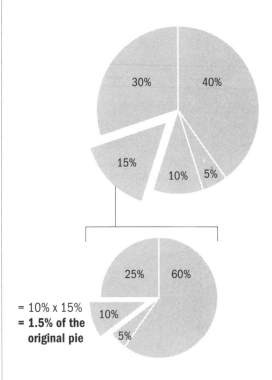

= 10% x 15%
= **1.5% of the original pie**

Go for a bar, instead of another pie

A segmented bar chart in general is more efficient than a pie chart at showing portions of a whole. It also allows for more segments than a pie without looking confusing. Be sure to label both the percentages and the actual values. It helps to put the segments in real terms.

One segmented bar within another is also a fine choice.

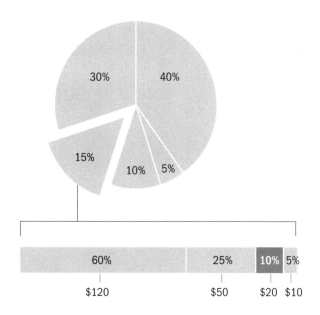

Proportional pies

Don't chart proportional pies in donut–pie chart style. The white circles inside the pies distort the ratio of the remaining area of the two pies.

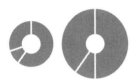

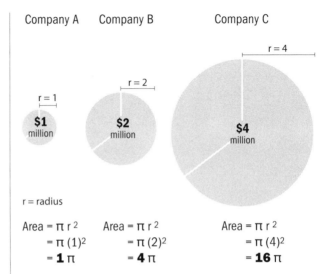

Company A   Company B   Company C

r = 1

$1 million

r = 2

$2 million

r = 4

$4 million

r = radius

Area = π r²   Area = π r²   Area = π r²
      = π (1)²   = π (2)²   = π (4)²
      = **1** π   = **4** π   = **16** π

Incorrect proportion based on radius

A common mistake is to represent the relative size of the circles based on their radii.

■ Relative radius of the three circles: 1, 2 and 4

■ Actual proportion of the three circles: 1, 4 and 16

In this example, the circles are drawn based on their relative radii. The picture grossly overstates company C, since the area of the circle that represents company C is 16 times that of company A. In reality, company C is only four times that of company A.

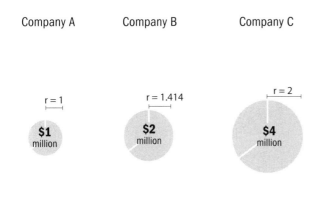

Company A	Company B	Company C
r = 1	r = 1.414	r = 2
$1 million	$2 million	$4 million

Area = π r²   Area = π r²   Area = π r²

$= \pi (1)^2$ $= \pi (1.414)^2$ $= \pi (2)^2$

$= \mathbf{1} \pi$ $= \mathbf{2} \pi$ $= \mathbf{4} \pi$

Correct proportion based on area

Remember geometry?
Area = π r². Proportional pies should always be calculated based on surface area.

■ Relative radius of the three circles: 1, 1.414 and 2

■ Actual proportion of the three circles: 1, 2 and 4

Based on the area of the circles, the three pies correctly represent the relative size of the three companies — $1 million, $2 million and $4 million.

Proportional pies concisely display two levels of information: the relative aggregate values between two or more pies, and the share of the segments within each pie.

Two pies of the same size can be used to represent different aggregate values, as long as they are clearly labeled.

Total revenue: Total revenue:
$2 million $4 million

Grid lines

Don't resort to a table unless a huge amount of data has to be included and space is limited. Rows of numbers do not have any visual impact. It requires a lot of work for the reader to compare and contrast the data.

Unhelpful grids

A large table using grid lines or alternating gray to separate each entry can be very daunting. The busy grid lines distract the reader from the data.

In a small table, alternating gray background or grid lines for every entry is unnecessary. The eyes can easily follow the numbers across the table.

Name	Data	Data	Data	Data	Data	Data
Company A	0.0	0.0	0.0	0.0	0.0	0.0
Company B	0.0	0.0	0.0	0.0	0.0	0.0
Company C	0.0	0.0	0.0	0.0	0.0	0.0
Company D	0.0	0.0	0.0	0.0	0.0	0.0
Company E	0.0	0.0	0.0	0.0	0.0	0.0
Company F	0.0	0.0	0.0	0.0	0.0	0.0
Company G	0.0	0.0	0.0	0.0	0.0	0.0
Company H	0.0	0.0	0.0	0.0	0.0	0.0

Name	Data	Data	Data	Data	Data	Data
Company A	0.0	0.0	0.0	0.0	0.0	0.0
Company B	0.0	0.0	0.0	0.0	0.0	0.0
Company C	0.0	0.0	0.0	0.0	0.0	0.0
Company D	0.0	0.0	0.0	0.0	0.0	0.0
Company E	0.0	0.0	0.0	0.0	0.0	0.0
Company F	0.0	0.0	0.0	0.0	0.0	0.0
Company G	0.0	0.0	0.0	0.0	0.0	0.0
Company H	0.0	0.0	0.0	0.0	0.0	0.0

Name	Data	Data	Data	Data	Data	Data
Company A	0.0	0.0	0.0	0.0	0.0	0.0
Company B	0.0	0.0	0.0	0.0	0.0	0.0
Company C	0.0	0.0	0.0	0.0	0.0	0.0
Company D	0.0	0.0	0.0	0.0	0.0	0.0
Company E	0.0	0.0	0.0	0.0	0.0	0.0
Company F	0.0	0.0	0.0	0.0	0.0	0.0
Company G	0.0	0.0	0.0	0.0	0.0	0.0
Company H	0.0	0.0	0.0	0.0	0.0	0.0

Optimal visual guides

Use thin rules after every three to five entries to help the reader follow the numbers across a table. A wide table needs a rule every three lines. A narrow table with two columns of numbers does not require any guides. Shading can be used to highlight a column of data or an entry.

Name	Data	Data	Data	Data	Data	Data
Company A	0.0	0.0	0.0	12.0	0.0	0.0
Company B	0.0	0.0	0.0	11.0	0.0	0.0
Company C	0.0	0.0	0.0	10.0	0.0	0.0
Company D	0.0	0.0	0.0	9.0	0.0	0.0
Company E	0.0	0.0	0.0	8.0	0.0	0.0
Company F	0.0	0.0	0.0	7.0	0.0	0.0
Company G	0.0	0.0	0.0	6.0	0.0	0.0
Company H	0.0	0.0	0.0	5.0	0.0	0.0
Company I	0.0	0.0	0.0	4.0	0.0	0.0
Company J	0.0	0.0	0.0	3.0	0.0	0.0
Company K	0.0	0.0	0.0	2.0	0.0	0.0
Company L	0.0	0.0	0.0	1.0	0.0	0.0

Chart in a table

Whenever space is available in a table, it is always helpful to chart the column of data that is the main message.

Name	Data	Data	Data		Data
Company A	0.0	0.0		12.0	0.0
Company B	0.0	0.0		11.0	0.0
Company C	0.0	0.0		10.0	0.0
Company D	0.0	0.0		9.0	0.0
Company E	0.0	0.0		8.0	0.0
Company F	0.0	0.0		7.0	0.0
Company G	0.0	0.0		6.0	0.0
Company H	0.0	0.0		5.0	0.0
Company I	0.0	0.0		4.0	0.0
Company J	0.0	0.0		3.0	0.0

Expressing quantitative and descriptive information in a tabular form is often the simplest method of presenting copious amounts of data. However, it should be used judiciously and as a last resort in most cases. **A chart is more memorable than a table of numbers.**

Numbers alignment and ordering

For a table with multiple data series, do not present the comparative data horizontally. It is easier for the reader to analyze data vertically.

Comparative data presented horizontally

	Company A	Company B	Company C
Sales	1	2	3
Profit/loss	11	12	13
Employees	210	220	230

Comparative data presented vertically

Name	Sales	Profit/ loss	Employees
Company A	1	11	210
Company B	2	12	220
Company C	3	13	230

Never align whole numbers flush left

Name	Data
Company A	1000
Company B	900
Company C	80
Company D	7

Never align decimals flush left or flush right

Name	Data
Company A	10.82
Company B	9.49
Company C	8
Company D	7.4

Name	Data
Company A	10.82
Company B	9.49
Company C	8
Company D	7.4

Never order entries randomly

Name	Data
Company A	4.1
Company C	5.1
Company D	2.1
Company B	3.1

Align whole numbers flush right

Name	Data
Company A	1000
Company B	900
Company C	80
Company D	7

Always align decimal numbers on the decimal point

Round off all figures to the same number of places after the decimal point, even whole numbers.

Example
Round off to one decimal point and align along the decimal point. Add ".0" after a round whole number so the decimals line up.

Name	Data
Company A	10.8
Company B	9.5
Company C	8.0
Company D	7.4

Order entries logically

In alphabetical order

Name	Data
Company A	4.1
Company B	3.1
Company C	5.1
Company D	2.1

Ranked by values

Name	Data
Company C	5.1
Company A	4.1
Company B	3.1
Company D	2.1

For small numbers, it is acceptable to center whole numbers.

Name	Data
Company A	10
Company B	9
Company C	8
Company D	7

In a table, It is only necessary to display the unit, such as a dollar sign or a percentage sign, once with the first entry. Just be sure to keep the numerals aligned.

Name	Data
Company A	$10
Company B	9
Company C	8
Company D	7

Name	Data
Company A	10%
Company B	9
Company C	8
Company D	7

Choice of icons

Avoid using partial icons in a pictogram. The purpose of a pictogram is to create a snapshot of the data. Partial icons add confusion.

The only exception is when using a square as an icon. A square works even if a small sliver of the unit is used.

 115

A truncated person or airplane is not only illegible but also disturbing.

 150

 150

Bad icons

Even though a pictogram is more visually engaging than a bar chart, it is less effective for comparing a large amount of data. A pictogram should be used only when comparing a few simple data series.

Icons in pictograms are not meant to be works of art. Icons that are visually interesting do not necessarily make good symbols for pictograms. A symbol with **too many details** hinders the readers from comparing the underlying data. When these symbols are used in multiples, they create a cluttered and busy picture.

Distracting variations

Don't use different versions of a symbol to represent the variables. The combinations can be very distracting and it is hard for the readers to compare the underlying data. The focus should be the information and not the drawing.

Existing home sales	New home sales	Homes foreclosed

12   11   3

Good icons

Icons or symbols are used to depict quantitative information in pictorial graphs. Pictograms can give a quick snapshot of quantity and volume, but are not suited to chart massive amounts of data. A bar chart is far more effective than a pictogram when comparing discrete quantities of several complex data series.

Icons used in pictograms should be simple. When these symbols are used in multiples, they still maintain a clear picture and present the data in an attractive and efficient way.

A test for determining a good icon:

☑ Simple.

☑ Symmetrical.

☑ Clear and crisp even when reduced to a small size.

☑ Roughly fits in a square.

One symbol, various shades

Use one symbol with different shades to represent the variables. The readers can focus on comparing and contrasting the data and not on the different styles of the icon.

Pictograms

Comparing quantities

If the data points are close together, do not use a pictogram. It is difficult to contrast and discern subtle differences in a busy picture.

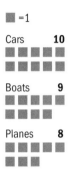

■ =1

Cars **10**

Boats **9**

Planes **8**

No shrinking houses or people

Don't chart quantitative information based on the area or height of an icon. Human eyes can't draw meaningful comparisons from irregular shapes. Stretching an icon in any dimension to represent the value only makes a chart look amateurish.

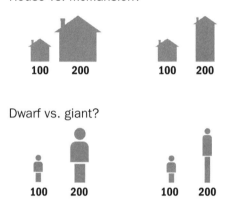

House vs. McMansion?

100   200   100   200

Dwarf vs. giant?

100   200   100   200

Avoid partial icons and awkward units

Avoid using partial icons. If most of the data points have to be represented by partial icons, a bar chart is more effective.

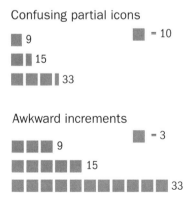

Confusing partial icons

■ 9   ■ = 10

■ 15

■ 33

Awkward increments

■ 9   ■ = 3

■ 15

■ 33

Comparing with multiple units

A pictogram takes the form of a bar chart and uses icons or symbols to visualize the data. Multiple units of a symbol are used to represent the discrete quantities.

An effective pictogram is visually engaging and gives a quick comparison of the variables.

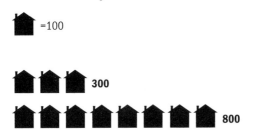

Always label the data values of a pictogram. Don't make the readers count.

Icons should be organized in groups of 5 or 10 to facilitate easy visual counting.

Unnatural grouping

Effective grouping

Natural units

In an effective pictogram, most data points should be multiples of a complete icon. Each icon should represent a natural counting increment, such as 1, 2, 5, 10, 50 and 100.

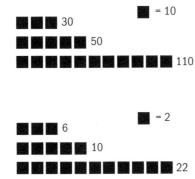

▼ Mapping and shading

Don't use patterns or cross-hatching to highlight an area. Use solid shades of black or another color.

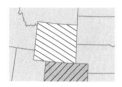

No mapping unless geography is relevant

Do not use a map to compare quantities or volume, unless geography is relevant to the message.

Suppose sales in New Jersey are three times that in Texas. Even if New Jersey is shaded black and Texas in light gray, the picture gives a different impression of the relative size of the business. A bar chart showing the sales figures is more effective.

Mapping change

For most business applications, a series of shaded maps can be very effective for comparing different conditions or showing change over time.

Example
Two maps show the market penetration of an Asian food product. The distribution grows with an increased presence of Asian consumers.

Last year ▨ Markets with sales of the Asian food product

This year ▨ Existing markets ■ New markets

Data maps can be powerful tools that analyze massive amounts of demographic information down to the metropolitan statistical area level. Highly sophisticated software and database expertise are required to execute such data maps.

Keep the outlines of a map simple, whether it is county, state or country. They are like the grid lines in a line or bar chart. They frame the information, but they are not the message.

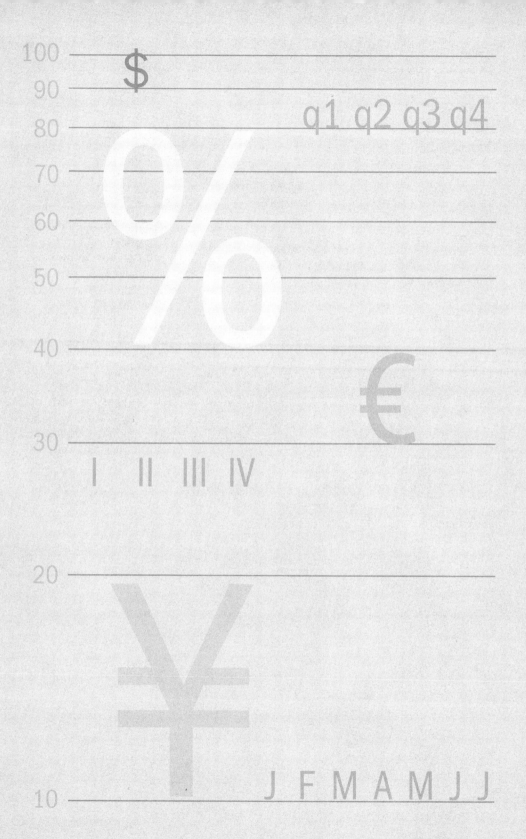

Ready Reference

Most of the math we use in charting is fundamental algebra and statistics. Yet most of us continue to make simple mistakes. Should we ever take an average of two percentages? How do we calculate percentage change: the new number minus the old number divided by the new number? Or divided by the old number? What is a log scale?

In addition to basic math skills, we also need knowledge of the market — the more, the better. What are the major stock indexes? How do we chart currency fluctuations that affect our global business?

These are all formulas and facts that save you time when you need to deliver quality work on a tight deadline. You will find them all here at your fingertips in this chapter.

Do the Math

Mean, median, mode

Which one to use?

The mean (average) is most useful when measuring the total impact of the complete data set since all the values are used to compute it. If the extreme outliers are not relevant, the mean may not be representative.

The median is useful for ranking outcomes. It is not influenced by outliers at the extremes of the data set. For instance, the median is a good representation for data on home prices and income level.

The mode helps focus on the typical outcome. It gives the value that users are most likely to see.

The **mean** is the simple average. It is the sum of all the values divided by the number of data points.

The **median** is the middle value in a distribution of data. Half of the sample is below that value and half is above. To find the median, the data has to be listed in numerical order. If the number of data points is an even number, the median is the average of the two middle values.

The **mode** is the value that occurs most often.

Example

A set of data showing the number of cars sold per day by nine divisions.

Mode = 7

7   7   7

4

3   3

2

1

11

Division   A   B   C   D   E   F   G   H   I

Half the sample below   **Median**   Half the sample above
= 4

$$\text{Mean} = \frac{1+2+3+3+4+7+7+7+11}{9} = 5$$

Standard deviation

Standard deviation shows how tightly the data is dispersed around the mean. A highly volatile stock has a high standard deviation.

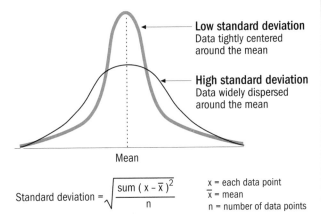

Low standard deviation
Data tightly centered around the mean

High standard deviation
Data widely dispersed around the mean

Mean

$$\text{Standard deviation} = \sqrt{\frac{\text{sum}\,(x - \bar{x})^2}{n}}$$

x = each data point
$\bar{x}$ = mean
n = number of data points

Example

One common business application for standard deviation is to represent the volatility of a series, based on percentage changes in prices.

Percent change in price	$x - \bar{x}$	$(x - \bar{x})^2$
3%	–5	25
1	–7	49
9	1	1
19	11	121
mean 8		*sum* 196

$$\text{Standard deviation} = \sqrt{\frac{196}{4}} = 7\%$$

The volatility is 7%.

For the quants:

Volatility is usually quoted on an annualized basis.

To calculate annualized volatility:

Daily standard deviation X $\sqrt{\text{Number of trading days in a year}}$

95

Do the Math

Probability

Probability can be interpreted as the relative number of occurrences. While one cannot predict with certainty the result of any one trial, the collective outcomes of a large number of trials can display some recurring patterns. Probability theory is widely used in many areas from actuarial estimates of mortality risk to clinical trials of new drugs.

Symmetric probability distributions

Symmetric distributions arise in many circumstances. For instance, test scores often fall along a bell-shaped curve.

Example. Toss 2 dice and plot the outcome. Enough trials will yield a bell curve:

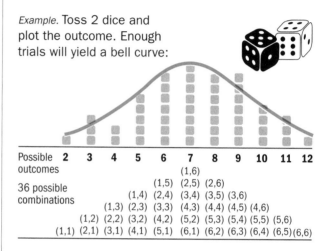

Possible outcomes	2	3	4	5	6	7	8	9	10	11	12
						(1,6)					
					(1,5)	(2,5)	(2,6)				
36 possible combinations				(1,4)	(2,4)	(3,4)	(3,5)	(3,6)			
			(1,3)	(2,3)	(3,3)	(4,3)	(4,4)	(4,5)	(4,6)		
		(1,2)	(2,2)	(3,2)	(4,2)	(5,2)	(5,3)	(5,4)	(5,5)	(5,6)	
	(1,1)	(2,1)	(3,1)	(4,1)	(5,1)	(6,1)	(6,2)	(6,3)	(6,4)	(6,5)	(6,6)

Fat-tails (kurtosis) indicate that extreme gains or losses are more frequent than the normal bell curve distribution might predict. The normal distribution is often used but it can significantly understate the risk of extreme events, for instance, the 1987 stock market crash.

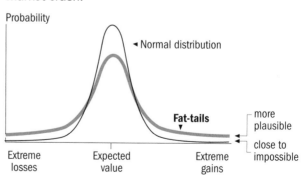

Skewed probability distributions

Skewed distributions occur in many practical applications, such as the distribution of income and credit default losses.

Uneven distribution of income

Personal income is one of the most studied and debated skewed distribution charts. It is used in socioeconomic studies that relate to inequality, poverty levels and economic growth.

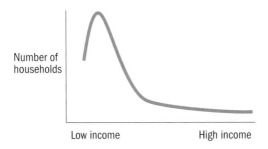

Number of households

Low income   High income

Small chance of a large loss

Bonds are unlikely to default, but there is a small chance of losing principal during the holding period.

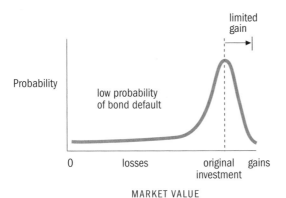

limited gain

Probability

low probability of bond default

0   losses   original   gains
                      investment

MARKET VALUE

Psychology of risk

The risk taker believes in the one-in-a-million chance of winning the lottery. The risk averse person worries about the slim chance of getting hit by lightning.

They both are motivated by outlier scenarios. They "live" in the tails of the distribution.

Do the Math

Average vs. weighted average

The Dow Jones Industrial Average is a price-weighted index. The index is therefore affected by the changes in the components' stock prices.

Weighted averages can improve upon simple averages by making the significant data points count for more. Be sure to use judgment in assigning importance. For instance, weights can be based on length of time, volume or monetary value. Weights need not be linear.

Example

The simple average of stock prices may include unrepresentative data from thin trading periods. Weighting the average based on volume corrects this bias.

Share prices	Trading volume	Price x Volume
$22	700 shares	15,400
19	1,000	19,000
15	200	3,000
18	400	7,200
16	300	4,800
sum 90	2,600	49,400

Simple average

$$= \frac{\text{sum(share price)}}{5}$$

$$= \frac{90}{5}$$

$$= \$18$$

Volume-weighted average

$$= \frac{\text{sum(share price x volume)}}{\text{total volume}}$$

$$= \frac{49,400}{2,600}$$

$$= \$19$$

Volume-weighted average price

Occasionally, buyers and sellers agree to execute their transactions at the volume-weighted average price, known as a VWAP trade.

Moving average

When a series is volatile, a moving average can help illustrate the underlying trend.

Example

A 4-day moving average of a volatile data series

Data series	Formula	Moving average
1		
4		
2		
8	(1+4+2+8)/4	3.75
3	(4+2+8+3)/4	4.25
12	(2+8+3+12)/4	6.25
4	(8+3+12+4)/4	6.75
16	(3+12+4+16)/4	8.75
5	(12+4+16+5)/4	9.25
16	(4+16+5+16)/4	10.25
9	(16+5+16+9)/4	11.50

The moving average can be plotted at either the midpoint or the endpoint of the data used to compute the average.

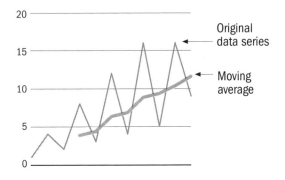

Original data series

Moving average

Do the Math

Logarithmic scale

Perception of time is not linear. In our mind, time speeds up the farther into the future we go. One year from today definitely feels closer than two years away. On the other hand, 10 years from today feels about the same as 11 years away. Both periods are one year apart, but we perceive them differently. Using a log scale to show time on the x-axis reflects that perceived duration.

X-axis log scale

A log scale allows you to include values that span many orders of magnitude.

We naturally are more interested in events closer to the present. Using a log scale for the timeline on the x-axis allows you to show more detail in the short term on the chart.

Example
The yield curve of Treasury bills, notes and bonds

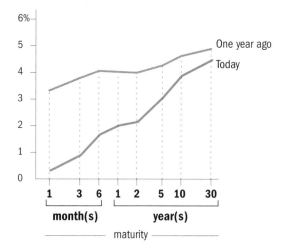

Y-axis log scale

Setting the y-axis on a log scale adjusts the grid lines so that incremental change at different values of the y-axis reflects its relative significance.

Example

A y-axis log scale can reflect a 10-point increase that has a much bigger impact when the index is at 10 than at 100. The same 10-point increase at 1,000 is negligible.

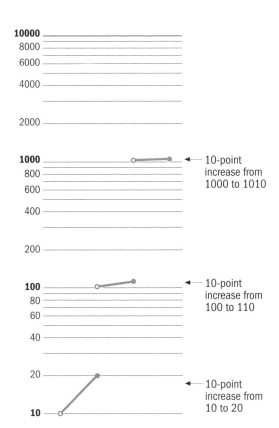

A y-axis log scale is most useful when plotting stocks or indexes over a long time horizon.

A logarithmic scale can use any base. In most graphics, base 10 is practical and intuitive.

$$\log_{10}10 = 1$$

$$\log_{10}50 = 1.7$$

$$\log_{10}100 = 2$$

$$\log_{10}500 = 2.7$$

$$\log_{10}1000 = 3$$

$$\log_{10}5000 = 3.7$$

$$\log_{10}10000 = 4$$

Do the Math

Comparable scales

When comparing and contrasting two or more data series, it is important to chart them on comparable scales. Readers expect **a flat line for small increases and a steeper slope for bigger increases.** The example below illustrates how comparable y-axis scales can give an accurate picture of the relative performance of two stocks.

Example

Stock A increased from $20 to $25. It is a 25% increase.

Stock B increased from $100 to $105. It is a 5% increase.

Noncomparable scales
Even though both stocks increase by $5, the charts are misleading when a 25% increase in the stock price is visually the same as a 5% increase.

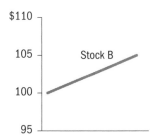

Percentage changes
Stock A with a 25% increase is a steep line. Stock B with a 5% increase is a much flatter line.

	Stock A	Stock B
Year 0	$20	$100
Year 1	$25	$105
Percentage change	+25%	+5%

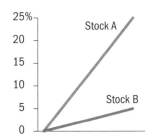

Comparable scales
Adjust the y-axis scales to reflect the relative slopes of the two lines. The picture immediately shows stock A outperformed stock B.

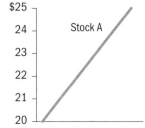

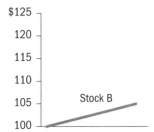

Deriving comparable scales step by step

The trading range of stock P is from $21 to $24, while stock Q ranges from $105 to $110.

1 Calculate which trading range is larger in percentage terms and determine the scale for that chart first. The range of stock P is about 14% while stock Q's range is less than 5%.

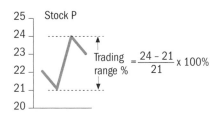

$$\text{Trading range \%} = \frac{24 - 21}{21} \times 100\%$$

2 Set the bottom value of the scale of the other chart using natural counting increments, such as 1, 2, 5, 10, 50 and 100.

Stock Q

100

3 Calculate the ratio between the bottom values of the two scales.

4 Multiply the top value of the first scale by the same ratio to get the top value of the other scale.

5 Double check the comparable scales by verifying that the percentage change between the top and bottom values of each scale is the same.

Both graphs are now on comparable scales that show the relative performance of the two stocks clearly.

103

Do the Math

Percentage change

When the new value is smaller than the original value, the result is a percentage decrease.

Example
If the value changes from 100 to 90,

Percentage change

$= \dfrac{90 - 100}{100}$ x 100%

$= -10\%$

The change in values can be expressed as a percentage change from the original value.

Percentage change $= \dfrac{\text{New number} - \text{Old number}}{\text{Old number}}$ x 100%

Example

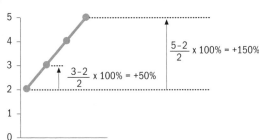

When calculating percentage changes from a data series, a different starting point will yield different numerical values for the percentage changes.

Example

		Percent change since	
	Data	January	February
Jan.	10	0%	
Feb.	15	+50	0%
March	12	+20	-20
April	6	-40	-60
May	9	-10	-40

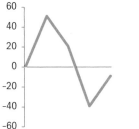

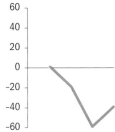

Re-indexing to 100 or 0

It is more intuitive to gauge the change when the baseline is 0 or 100. For example, it is obvious that the change from 100 to 113 is a 13% increase. However, a 13% increase from 123 to 139 is not immediate.

We are accustomed to the round multiples of 10, so it is also relevant to rebase data to 1,000 or 10,000 depending on the subject. For instance, the performance of a stock can be charted in terms of a $10,000 initial investment.

Example

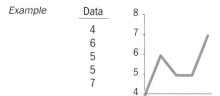

Data
4
6
5
5
7

Re-indexing to 100 is scaling the data to start at 100.

(Current value/Initial value) x 100

Data	Formula	Re-indexed to 100
4	(4/4) x 100	100
6	(6/4) x 100	150
5	(5/4) x 100	125
5	(5/4) x 100	125
7	(7/4) x 100	175

Rebasing to 0 essentially gives the percentage change from the first data point. Here's another way to calculate it.

[(Current value/Initial value) x 100] – 100

Data	Formula	Rebased to 0
4	[(4/4) x 100] – 100	0
6	[(6/4) x 100] – 100	50
5	[(5/4) x 100] – 100	25
5	[(5/4) x 100] – 100	25
7	[(7/4) x 100] – 100	75

Percentages

Expressing percentages

There are several ways to express a change in values. For example, an increase from 2 to 6 can be described as follows:

The value triples from 2 to 6.

The value increases by 200%.

Percentages vs. Percentage points vs. Basis points

The difference between two percentages is expressed in percentage points or basis points.

1 percentage point = 100 basis points

Example

$$2.00\%$$
$$\text{less } 1.75\%$$
$$= 0.25 \text{ percentage points}$$
$$= 25 \text{ basis points}$$

Baseline number

It is very important to include a baseline number when expressing percentage change. For example, describe a 20% change as a 20% increase **from $10** or 20% increase **to $12**. Presenting the percentage number without reference to a base number is ambiguous. We would not give directions such as "drive 20 miles" without noting the direction north or south.

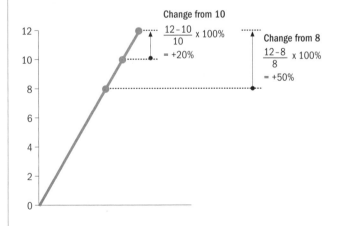

Change from 10

$$\frac{12-10}{10} \times 100\%$$
$$= +20\%$$

Change from 8

$$\frac{12-8}{8} \times 100\%$$
$$= +50\%$$

Absolute values vs. percentage changes

Same curve, different message

Charting the absolute values or the percentage changes from the initial data point yields the same shape for the graphs. The chart plotting the percentage changes accentuates the changes from the baseline.

Example
Plotting the percentage changes brings the line into the negative territory, which accentuates the drop in prices.

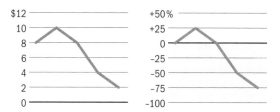

Don't compare percentage changes for two entities that are not comparable in size. For example, comparing the percentage change in revenue of a large company with $100 million in revenue to a small company with only $10,000 is misleading. Even a 100% increase in sales for that small company can still be a small sliver of the total market.

Comparing two or more data series

When comparing different data series, plotting percentage changes from the initial data point can be more telling than absolute values.

Example
Both stock A and stock B increase by $10 in the same period. By plotting the percentage changes from the same start date, the chart immediately conveys stock A outperformed stock B.

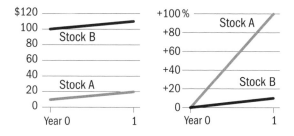

Percentages

Percent of a percentage

Don't make your readers work. Do the math for them.

$$A\% \text{ of } B\% = \frac{A}{100} \times B\%$$

Example 1
50% of 8% = 50/100 x 8% = 4%

Example 2
Total number of units = 100

A owns 70%
= 70 units

B owns 30%
= 30 units

Each pays 10% fee:

10% fee of 70%
= 10/100 x 70%
= 7%

10% fee of 30%
= 10/100 x 30%
= 3%

A pays 7 units
or 7% of 100 units

B pays 3 units
or 3% of 100 units

Don't average percentages

When it comes to averaging, percentages should not be treated like ordinary numbers. You must always **go back to the original data source to recalculate a new percentage.**

Myth Average of A% and B% $= \dfrac{A + B}{2}$ %

$$A\% = \frac{c}{e} \qquad B\% = \frac{d}{f}$$

$$\text{New percentage} = \frac{c + d}{e + f} \times 100\%$$

Example 1

The average of 10% and 14% is NOT 12%.

Going back to the original data source:

$$10\% = 30/300; \quad 14\% = 28/200$$

$$\text{New percentage} = \frac{30 + 28}{300 + 200} \times 100\% = 11.6\%$$

Example 2

The percent of population in each state that holds bank Z credit card:

Alabama 12.3%
Alaska   3.3%
:
:
Wyoming   4.1%

$$\text{National average} \neq \frac{(12.3 + 3.3 + \cdots + 4.1)\%}{50}$$

$$\text{National market} = \frac{\text{Sum of credit card Z holders in 50 states}}{\text{Total population}} \times 100\%$$

Exception: It is okay to average percentages if they are calculated from the same base. For example, the average grade of a class is the simple average of the students' grades, since they are all based on 100%.

Words

In tables, spell out the full name of the companies and organizations. Don't assume readers know the acronyms. The Bureau of Labor Statistics is still more informative than BLS. An acronym can be used only when it is so widely recognized that it has replaced the full name in the public eye, such as IBM for International Business Machines.

Months

On the x-axis, either use the first three letters or present the names of the months as follows.

Jan.	Feb.	March	April	May	June
July	Aug.	Sept.	Oct.	Nov.	Dec.

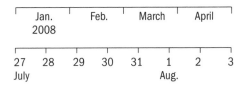

When charting a time period six months or longer, use only the first initial.

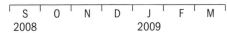

In tables, spell out the months when using them alone or with a year, for example, January 2009. Don't separate the year with a comma. For a specific date, abbreviate or spell out the months as shown above and set off the year with a comma, for example, Jan. 1, 2009.

State and city names

In tables, spell out the names of the 50 U.S. states when they stand alone without a city name.
U.S. city names should be used in conjunction with the state name. Add a comma after the city name, for example, Louisville, Ky. Spell out Alaska, Hawaii, Idaho, Iowa, Maine, Ohio, Texas and Utah. Abbreviate others as listed.

Ala.	Ariz.	Ark.	Calif.	Colo.	Conn.	Del.
Fla.	Ga.	Ill.	Ind.	Kan.	Ky.	La.
Mass.	Md.	Mich.	Minn.	Miss.	Mo.	Mont.
N.C.	N.D.	N.H.	N.J.	N.M.	N.Y.	Neb.
Nev.	Okla.	Ore.	Pa.	R.I.	S.C.	S.D.
Tenn.	Va.	Vt.	W.Va.	Wash.	Wis.	Wyo.

Numerals

Years
Write out the full year when there is space. When space is limited, the first reference should be in full and the rest in two digits.

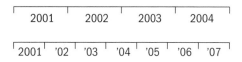

| 2001 | 2002 | 2003 | 2004 |

| 2001 | '02 | '03 | '04 | '05 | '06 | '07 |

In the description that accompanies a chart, spell out numbers one to twelve. For figures 13 or higher, use numerals. For all percentage numbers, it is more readable to use numeral figures rather than words, such as 1% and 12%.

Quarters
Always indicate the year with quarterly figures.

| q1 | q2 | q3 | q4 |

2001

| I | II | III | IV |

2001

Whole numbers and decimals
Never center numbers or align numbers flush left.

3	5.1	7.1
4	6.1	8.1
11	12.1	9.**0**

Whole numbers
Flush right

Decimals
Align on decimal point

Whole numbers and decimals
Add ".0" after a round whole number so decimals line up

Units
Keep the units to the highest reasonable denomination. Don't make the reader do the math.

Correct	Incorrect
$3 billion	$3,000 million
2	2,000
1	1,000
0	0

Money

Major stock indexes

The stock market activity is reported daily in market indexes.
These indexes reflect investors' sentiment. Since no single index
can represent a complete picture of the economy, some countries
have several indexes to track different sectors of the market.

North America

Nation	Main market indexes
U.S.	Dow Jones Industrial Average
	Nasdaq Composite
	Standard & Poor's 500
	Russell 2000
	Dow Jones Wilshire 5000
Canada	S&P/TSX Composite

Latin America

Brazil	Bovespa
Chile	IPSA
Colombia	IGBC General
Mexico	IPC All Share

Asia/Pacific

Australia	S&P/ASX 200
China	Shanghai Composite
Hong Kong	Hang Seng
India	Bombay Sensex
Indonesia	Jakarta Composite
Japan	Nikkei Stock Average
Malaysia	Kuala Lumpur Composite
Singapore	Straits Times
South Korea	KOSPI
Taiwan	Weighted
Thailand	SET

Europe

Nation	Main market indexes
All Europe	Dow Jones Euro Stoxx 50
Belgium	Bel 20
Britain	FTSE 100
Denmark	OMX Copenhagen 20
Finland	OMX Helsinki 25
France	CAC 40
Germany	Xetra DAX
Greece	Athens General
Italy	S&P/MIB
Luxembourg	LuxX
Netherlands	AEX
Norway	OSE All Share
Poland	WIG
Portugal	PSI 20
Russia	RTS
Spain	IBEX 35
Sweden	OMX Stockholm 30
Switzerland	Swiss Market
Turkey	ISE National 100

Africa/Middle East

Egypt	CASE 30
Israel	Tel Aviv 25
South Africa	FTSE/JSE All Share

Source: WSJ Market Data Group

Dow Jones Industrial Average

A chart showing the daily closes of the Dow in the 52-week period leading up to March 29, 1999.

"The Dow" is the world's most frequently quoted and longest-serving market indicator of its kind, measuring the U.S. market since its creation by Charles Dow in 1896. The index first closed above the 10,000 point milestone on March 29, 1999.

The Dow at one-minute interval

A minute-by-minute chart of the Dow shows the movements of the stock market throughout a one-day trading period.

Source: WSJ Market Data Group

Measuring performance

The price return shows the growth in the value of a stock or an index excluding dividends. An investor can see a more accurate picture of an index's actual investment return using a total return index. A total return index captures both the price change and the reinvested dividends.

Price return vs. Total return

To illustrate the total return of investment in the index, the dividends of the component stocks have to be included. Typically, the dividend is reinvested in the same index or held in cash.

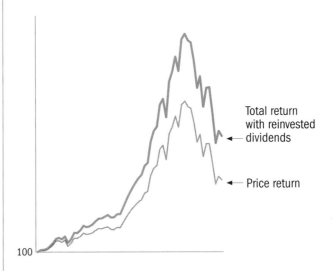

Total return with reinvested dividends

Price return

100

Showing relative performance

To show the performance of a stock against an index and its peer group, it is common to plot the return with reinvested dividends of a hypothetical $100 investment in each of them. The original data series was rebased to 100.

Stock indexes are averages weighted by price or by market capitalization or other characteristics of the component stocks.

See page 98 for weighted average.

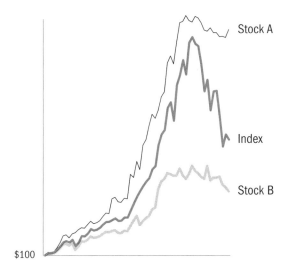

Money

Arithmetic vs. geometric rate of return

Each year's investment return is dependent on prior years' return. For instance, if you have a big gain one year, you have much more capital to generate returns during the following years, and vice versa. Geometric return is therefore a more accurate measurement of how an investment does over a period of time.

Arithmetic rate of return
Simple average of the rate of return in each year

Geometric rate of return
Compounded rate of return of initial investment

Example
How well did stock A perform?

Year	Price	Annual rate of return
0	$100	
1	150	+50%
2	75	–50
3	90	+20
4	72	–20

Arithmetic return = Average of annual rates of return
= (+50% – 50% + 20% – 20%) /4
= 0%

Geometic return = Annualized appreciation over four years

$$= \sqrt[4]{\frac{72}{100}} - 1 = -7.9\%$$

This means stock A loses 7.9% per year.

How the math works:

Year	Annualized rate	Stock value
0		$100
1	– 7.9%	92
2	– 7.9%	85
3	– 7.9%	78
4	– 7.9%	72

Example

Imagine an investment of $10,000 growing at a 20% average rate of return.

Year	Return
1	–20%
2	+50
3	+100
4	–50

Average rate of return: ➝ +20% or 0.2

Myth It would be a mistake to believe the investment is compounding at 20% a year:

$$\$10{,}000 \times (1 + 0.2)^4 = \$20{,}736$$

Reality The investment compounds at 4.7%. Based on the geometric return, the account will be worth only $12,000. Compounding the arithmetic return grossly overstates the growth by more than $8,000.

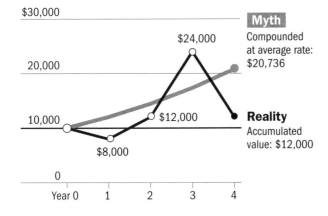

For the quants:

The difference between arithmetic return and geometric return is due to the dispersion of annual returns.

Geometric return

$$= \begin{array}{c} \textbf{Arithmetic} \\ \textbf{return} \end{array} - \begin{array}{c} \text{Adjustment} \\ \text{factor} \end{array}$$

where adjustment factor

$$= \dfrac{\left(\begin{array}{c}\text{Standard deviation} \\ \text{of annual returns}\end{array}\right)^2}{2}$$

The adjustment factor is a numerical approximation to the exact difference between the two.

Money

Expressing currencies

There is a large and active market in foreign exchange. Anyone involved in a global enterprise will need to use the standard conventions for translating results into different currencies. Here's a sample table of spot exchange rates.

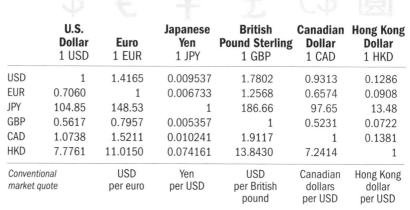

	U.S. Dollar 1 USD	Euro 1 EUR	Japanese Yen 1 JPY	British Pound Sterling 1 GBP	Canadian Dollar 1 CAD	Hong Kong Dollar 1 HKD
USD	1	1.4165	0.009537	1.7802	0.9313	0.1286
EUR	0.7060	1	0.006733	1.2568	0.6574	0.0908
JPY	104.85	148.53	1	186.66	97.65	13.48
GBP	0.5617	0.7957	0.005357	1	0.5231	0.0722
CAD	1.0738	1.5211	0.010241	1.9117	1	0.1381
HKD	7.7761	11.0150	0.074161	13.8430	7.2414	1
Conventional *market quote*		USD per euro	Yen per USD	USD per British pound	Canadian dollars per USD	Hong Kong dollar per USD

Note: Traders' screens often do not align numbers on decimal points. The number of decimal points are based on conventional quotes.

Converting currencies

When converting a foreign currency into U.S. dollars, either multiply or divide the foreign currency by the exchange rate, depending on the standard conventions for each rate. Since currencies fluctuate, use the exchange rate that is relevant to the time period.

Example. Converting 100 Canadian dollars into U.S. dollars

Convention	Exchange rate	Algebra	Conversion
Currency unit per U.S. dollar	C$1.0738 = US $1	1.0738 = 1 100 = ? = (100 x 1) / 1.0738	Divide by the exchange rate C$100 / 1.0738 C$100 = US $93.13

Example. Converting 100 British pounds into U.S. dollars

Convention	Exchange rate	Algebra	Conversion
U.S. dollar per currency unit	US$1.7802 = £1	1 = 1.7802 100 = ? = (100 x 1.7802) / 1	Multiply by the exchange rate £100 x 1.7802 £100 = US $178.02

Online: Currencies rates are available at http://wsjmarkets.com

A windfall gain

Exchange rates need to be taken into consideration when presenting financial data for overseas operations.

When presenting assets and liabilities such as inventory and loans, use the **exchange rate at the end of each period** (e.g. Dec. 31) to show the value accumulated to date.

When presenting profits and losses, use the **average exchange rate** during each period to show the impact of currency on the performance during that period.

For the inquisitive:

In accounting, a fudge factor known as the cumulative translation adjustment (CTA) is used to reconcile the differences that arise from using average and end-of-period exchange rates together.

Example. Profit of a German subsidiary

Period	Quarterly profit (million)	Average exchange rate	Profit in U.S. dollar (million)
q1	5 euro	1 euro = US$1.00	$ 5.0
q2	6	1 euro = US$1.10	6.6
q3	7	1 euro = US$1.20	8.4
q4	8	1 euro = US$1.30	10.4

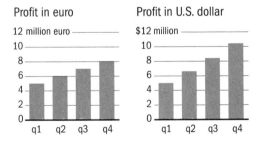

When the euro gets stronger, the profit in U.S. dollars reflects a windfall gain.

Money

Currency charts

It is important to chart currencies in a way that is intuitive for the readers. Readers expect to see **an upward trend line as the currency strengthens and a downward trend line as the currency weakens.**

Conventional market quote

- U.S. dollar per euro
- Yen per U.S. dollar
- U.S. dollar per British pound
- Canadian dollar per U.S. dollar
- Hong Kong dollar per U.S. dollar

With globalization, many business presentations include currency charts to reflect how currency fluctuations are affecting performance.

Strength/weakness of the U.S. dollar
against the other currency

If the focus of the message is linked to the U.S. dollar, the chart should show the number of foreign currency units $1 can buy.

Example
The U.S. dollar strengthens against the yen, i.e. $1 buys more yen. The line trends up to show a stronger dollar.

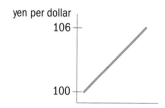

The U.S. dollar weakens against the yen, i.e. $1 buys fewer yen. The line slopes down to show a weaker dollar.

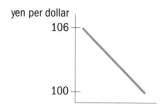

Strength/weakness of a foreign currency
against the U.S. dollar

If the focus of the message is linked to the foreign currency, the chart should show how many U.S. dollars one unit of foreign currency can buy.

Example
The euro strengthens against the U.S. dollar, i.e. 1 euro buys more dollars. The line trends up to show a stronger euro.

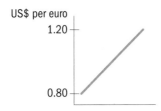

The euro weakens against the U.S. dollar, i.e. 1 euro buys fewer dollars. The line slopes down to show a weaker euro.

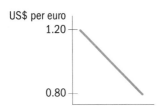

Inverse scale

There are times when adhering to the conventional market quote can lead to a chart with an upward trend for a weakening currency and vice versa. An inverse scale can turn the line to give an intuitive presentation.

Example
The focus of the message is the U.S. dollar and the currency convention is dollars per euro. An inverse scale will show a stronger dollar with an upward trend. It costs fewer dollars to buy 1 euro.

An inverse scale should only be used for a sophisticated audience and should be clearly footnoted.

Missing Data?

Big
Numbers

Small Change

Coloring with black ink

Comparable
Scales

CHAPTER 4

Tricky Situations

Raw data is like a diamond in the rough — it needs to be polished and mounted before it can be shown to the world. There are times when you can present just your data. But, in most instances, you should be prepared to reorganize your information so as to convey your intended message effectively.

In the real world, unexpected issues are bound to arise. Should you throw out a data set if you are missing some data points? How do you present a small increase from a large base fairly? What is the most effective way to visually compare a stock that trades in the $10 range versus one in the $100 range? When color is not available to you, how do you use black ink to your advantage?

Finding the right solution within a particular set of parameters comes down to judgment and experience. In this chapter, I shed light on these topics to provide you with a foundation for working through even more complicated situations.

Is it still worth charting?

After you have exhausted all your resources and still find your data set incomplete, should you still chart your information? If your objective is to show a broad trend and you are missing only a few data points, it is still worthwhile to plot the data.

Assess whether the chart presents an unbiased story overall despite missing data points.

It is acceptable to combine several sources to complete a data set, as long as the sources have the same general methodology for data collection.

One or two data points missing

In most cases, a chart with one or two missing data points still has value. The exception is when the missing data point is crucial to your message, for instance, December sales figures of a toy store.

For a bar chart, leave a space for the missing data point. Make a footnote. If more than two out of ten data points are missing, do not make a bar chart.

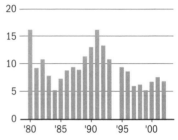

Note: 1994 data is unavailable.

For a line chart with a long data series, span the gap and continue the line. Since the objective is to show a trend, a few missing data points do not have a big effect.

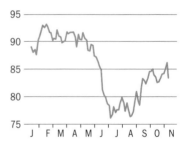

For a line chart with a short data series, span the gap and mark the data points. Do not plot the line if more than two out of ten data points are missing.

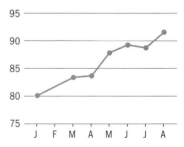

Scattered data points

If a data series has several missing data points, select a sample of directly relevant data points that convey the message. Research additional data to substantiate the chart.

Example

Plot the most recent value and select a historical data point that is directly relevant to the message, for instance the year that the product was first launched.

Do not make a pie chart if the data for any one segment is unavailable. A pie chart always represents a whole and adds up to 100%.

Revenue in millions of dollars

2010	$200
2007	$100

In addition, incorporate new information, such as revenue breakdown by division, to make the chart more illuminating.

Revenue by division

2010 Revenue: $200 million

A	B	C	D
$100	$50	$40	$10

2007 Revenue: $100 million

A	B	C	D
$25	$25	$25	$25

Big Numbers, Small Change

Accentuate without exaggeration

Always plot vertical bars from a zero baseline. Vertical bars that start at values other than zero exaggerate the changes, obscure the discrete total value of each bar and make comparison of the data difficult.

In the example below, the chart appears to show that the value in 2009 is six times that of 2008. In reality, it is only twice the value of the previous year. The reader cannot infer the truth by visual inspection of the height of the two bars.

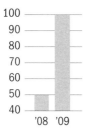

Show changes vs. absolute values

If your data points are large numbers or are close in value, the vertical bars can be indistinguishable in height. In such instances it may be more effective to plot the point changes or percentage changes. Do not change a bar chart to a line chart to exaggerate a trend. Always use bars to represent discrete quantities.

Example

Year	Revenue	Change from a year ago
2004	$ 80 million	
2005	85	+$ 5 million
2006	92	+ 7
2007	100	+ 8

Plotting the absolute values shows the actual revenues.

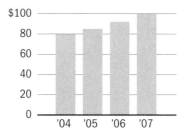

Plotting the changes from a year ago accentuates the increase in revenue from year to year.

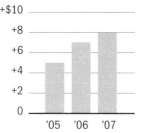

126

Show recent changes with historical perspective

Sometimes a chart needs to serve dual purposes — to show a historical trend and to show recent peaks or troughs. In a chart with a long time horizon, it could be difficult to see small changes in the latest data points. In such instances, plot the historical data series with an additional chart or an inset to magnify the points of interest.

In the example below, the chart plotting the most recent data points highlights that the value drops in half in the last five days.

The time frame for both the longer horizon chart and the close-up should directly relate to the message, whether it is a ten-year trend or a one-week period. The purpose for magnifying the recent data points is to show any significant changes that would otherwise be missed in the main chart. Do not zoom in for decorative purposes.

Two panels side by side

Magnifying visual effect

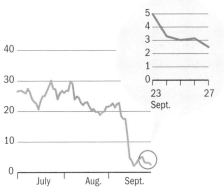

Comparable Scales

Ant vs. Elephant

Percentage changes are often more telling than absolute values, since investors can apply the percentage change to the dollar amount of their initial investment.

How to fairly compare the performance of a $10 stock to a $100 stock

A $10 increase for a $10 stock is not the same as a $10 increase for a $100 stock. The former doubles in value whereas the $100 stock increases by only 10%.

Plotting the percentage changes

Example	Year	Stock A	Stock B
	0	$10	$100
	1	$20	$110
	Percent change from a year ago	+100%	+10%

Plotting the actual values of the stocks is technically correct but it is impossible to judge visually the relative performance of the two stocks.

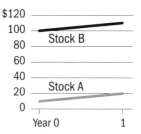

The chart below, on the other hand, immediately shows the $10 stock outperformed the $100 stock.

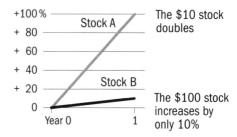

Choosing comparable scales

Sometimes, it is more relevant to show the actual values instead of the percentage changes. In such instances, plotting the charts on comparable scales is the only fair way to compare the data series.

A quick and easy method to derive comparable scales is to determine the upper and lower y-axis values that increase by the same percentage for both charts.

Example
The y-axis scale for the $10-range stock can go from $6 to $12 and the $100-range stock goes from $80 to $160. Both ranges increase by 100%.

Readers expect a flat line for small increases and a steeper slope for bigger increases. Plotting the charts on comparable scales helps create the right comparison.

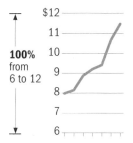

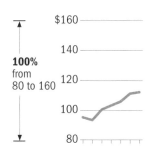

It is tempting to choose a scale from $90 to $120 for the $100-range stock. However, such a scale will exaggerate its relative performance to the $10-range stock.

Creating contrast and highlights

A graphic can be "colorful" even in black and white.
The use of different shades of black can create layers of texture. The contrast with light and dark shades can be used to emphasize the focal point.

The same shade of black can look different against a different shaded background. In the example below, the small squares in the center of the four panels are all 30% black, but they look different depending on the surrounding gray background.

0% black   20% black   55% black   100% black

 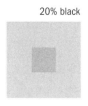 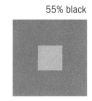 

Contrast and readability
There is a trade-off between contrast and readability. Too little contrast makes it hard to differentiate between elements. Too much contrast creates vibration that diminishes readability, such as images on a black background. Black text or graphics on a white or light-colored background is most legible.

Too much contrast

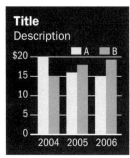

More legible

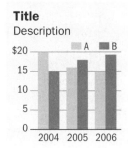

Highlighting with shades of black

Shades of black can be used to separate different levels of information. Sufficient contrast brings out the important message.

The important line is in black.

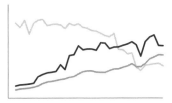

Determine visually, and not numerically, the graduating steps of gray. Strictly using equal increments of the percentage numbers may yield an uneven gray scale. Start with numerical steps and adjust visually.

Numerical steps yield an uneven gradation.

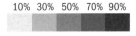

10% 30% 50% 70% 90%

The highlighted segment can either be a lighter shade or a darker shade.

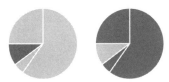

Adjust visually for a more effective gray scale.

10% 20% 38% 57% 90%

Moderate use of boldfaced type and shading can help emphasize the important data.

Name	Data	Data	Data	Data
Company A	0.0	0.0	**12.0**	0.0
Company B	0.0	0.0	**11.0**	0.0
Company C	0.0	0.0	**10.0**	0.0
Company D	0.0	0.0	**9.0**	0.0
Company E	0.0	0.0	**8.0**	0.0

A gray scale can be used to differentiate levels of gradation.

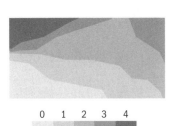

0 1 2 3 4

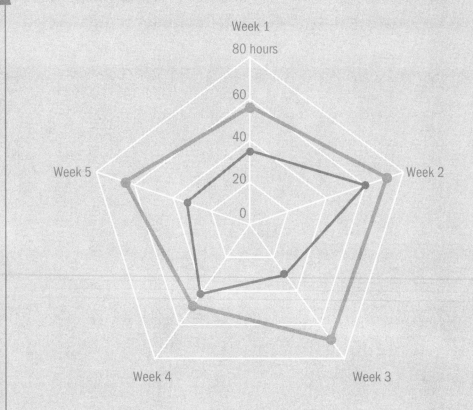

Week 1
80 hours

60

40

20

0

Week 5

Week 2

Week 4

Week 3

Days ahead of schedule
Amount under budget

Charting Your Course

Out in the corporate jungle, our project plan, budget illustration and progress report are vital navigation tools. They are our compass and North Star.

What's the most effective way to communicate with decision makers when we have five minutes of their time?

A concise graphic illustration creates focus and urgency for the audience and helps the team stay on track. Laying out the plan graphically often helps identify challenges ahead of time.

Drawing up a successful plan is planning for success.

Mapping It Out

Assembling your team

An **org chart** not only displays titles, but can also present functional roles that change with each project.

In presenting any organizational chart, keep the graphical elements simple. Avoid using frames around each name, which add no information. Keep the chart clean so the readers can focus on the interlocking relationships.

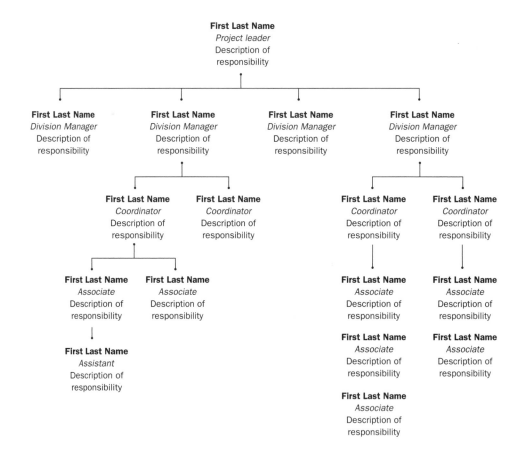

Drafting the blueprint

Simplify the mechanics of a **flow chart,** such as a transaction diagram or workflow, into its major components. It is not necessary to show all the alternatives in one diagram. It is best to show different phases of the process with modified versions of the original. Too many arrows weaving in and out can make the chart so convoluted that the reader is at a complete loss.

Example
A flow diagram of structured finance

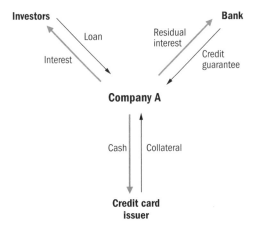

Color can be used to differentiate the direction of the arrows.

Avoid using boxes in flow diagrams. Only add as many graphic elements and as much complexity as needed. Help the readers focus on the flow of the arrows and not on the boxes.

Do not turn the type sideways to follow the arrow. Leave the type upright so the readers can easily read the labels without turning their heads.

Scheduling the work plan

A detailed **work plan** helps you anticipate potential roadblocks and reconcile competing priorities before a project begins.

Example
Description of all action items of each project in the time allotted

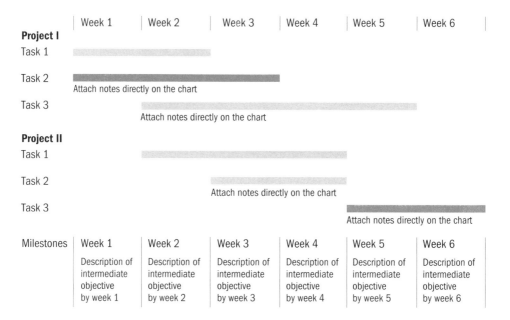

	Week 1	Week 2	Week 3	Week 4	Week 5	Week 6
Project I						
Task 1						
Task 2	Attach notes directly on the chart					
Task 3		Attach notes directly on the chart				
Project II						
Task 1						
Task 2			Attach notes directly on the chart			
Task 3					Attach notes directly on the chart	
Milestones	Week 1	Week 2	Week 3	Week 4	Week 5	Week 6
	Description of intermediate objective by week 1	Description of intermediate objective by week 2	Description of intermediate objective by week 3	Description of intermediate objective by week 4	Description of intermediate objective by week 5	Description of intermediate objective by week 6

You can use color to differentiate assignments to different groups or individuals or to signify the importance of the tasks. Summarize notes into key points and incorporate them in the chart. These work plans serve as an at-a-glance summary. Attaching the notes right on the timeline bars enables the reader to make quick and direct references without looking elsewhere on the page or, worse, flipping to other pages. Short notes should be shown on the chart. Follow-on notes should be reserved for items that require extensive and detailed explanation.

Tracking the competition

A visual **timeline** can drive home the effort required to meet management expectations, make trade-offs, and create the impetus for action.

Example
Timeline of product launches

Company A	Product A1	Product A2		Product A3			Product A4
	Brief description follows	Brief description follows		Brief description follows			Brief description follows
	2002	2003		2005			2008

Company B	Product B1	Product B2		Product B3	
	Brief description follows	Brief description follows		Brief description follows	
	2002	2003		2006	

Company C			Product C1	Product C2	Product C3
			Brief description follows	Brief description follows	Brief description follows
			2006	2007	2008

Color can be used to highlight competing products. When charting parallel timelines, all years should be aligned even if no milestones are posted. In doing so, it is sufficient to label only the dateline that has information.

Staying On Track

Communicating progress

No plan is perfect. A **progress report** helps reassess the situation and adapt strategies in order to stay on track.

Example
A progress report, when outlined with the impact on overall workflow and the action items required to keep the project on track, can create urgency and help redirect ineffective strategy.

Status ● Delayed ○ On track ● Completed

	Deadline	Team A	Team B	Impact on other work streams	Management action required
Task 1	Jan. 1	●	○		
Task 2	Feb. 2	○	●	Description of impact on other work streams	List action items required to adjust plan
Task 3	March 3*	●	○	Description of impact on other work streams	List action items required to adjust plan
Task 4	April 4	●	○		
Task 5	May 5	○	○		
Task 6	June 6	○	●	Description of impact on other work streams	List action items required to adjust plan

*Revised deadline

Color can be used to highlight tasks that are behind schedule. The pattern created can help decision makers assess whether this is due to a lack of resources or due to setting unrealistic targets. When color is not available, different shades of black can be just as effective.

Minimize the grid lines. Heavy grid lines will overpower the dots, which carry the main message.

Finding the big fish in your pond

Prioritizing is vital. Identify and focus on key items that have the biggest impact. A concise chart to identify high-priority projects that are underperforming can help managers focus on any important aspects of the project that need improvement.

Example
A status report showing larger icons for more important tasks can help direct resources to high-priority projects that need more work.

Status by color of circles   **Importance** by size of circles

| Not effective | Highly effective | | Low priority | High priority |

	Team A	Team B	Team C	Team D
Task 1	●	·	●	●
Task 2	·	●	●	●
Task 3	●	●	●	·
Task 4	●	●	·	●
Task 5	●	·	●	●
Task 6	●	●	●	●

Management communication may be dominated by good news about projects that are already on track (● ● ●) or their attention may be diverted by secondary initiatives (● ● ●). Both take time away from high-impact initiatives.

This status report allows managers to see that they should focus on projects that are important and are not as effective yet (● ●).

What goes around ...

A **spider chart** allows easier comparisons among all data points. This can be superior to ordinary bar charts, which emphasize sequential comparisons. Spider charts are most useful for illustrating recurring patterns in the data set.

Example
A spider chart is used to compare hours worked by two employees over a five-week period. The size of the polygon quickly indicates who worked the most overall, and the shape provides interweek comparisons.

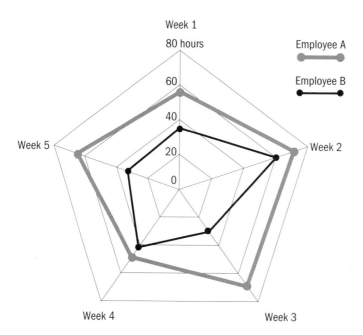

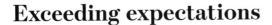

Exceeding expectations

The two most immediate questions for many project managers are:

- Are we on schedule?
- Are we on budget?

Plotting the schedule versus the budget is a simple and direct way to communicate to senior management.

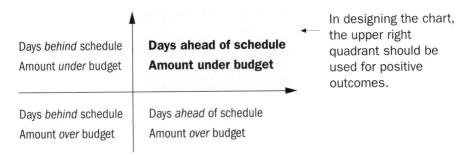

| Days *behind* schedule | **Days ahead of schedule** |
| Amount *under* budget | **Amount under budget** |

In designing the chart, the upper right quadrant should be used for positive outcomes.

| Days *behind* schedule | Days *ahead* of schedule |
| Amount *over* budget | Amount *over* budget |

Example

This chart provides a quick summary of where all the projects stand in terms of timeliness and cost savings. It's readily apparent that projects A and D exceed expectations.

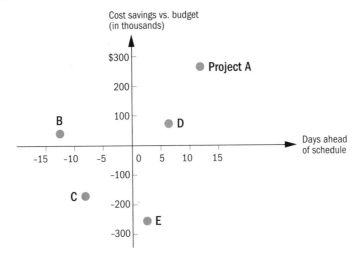

In Brief

Tell a compelling story with every chart by making a conscious choice of data set, presentation style and color scheme.

- ■ Put numbers in context.

- ■ Do the math for your readers. Decide whether percentage changes or absolute values give a more faithful representation.

- ■ Use as few font styles as possible. Use bold or italic only to differentiate, but not both at the same time.

- ■ Use color to convey information and not for decoration.

- ■ Work hard to make it effortless for your readers. Use natural increments for the y-axis scale. Include a zero baseline in all bar charts. Place the larger segments of a pie chart on the top at 12 o'clock.

Essentially, use as few graphical elements as possible to keep the visuals clean and crisp. Complexity should be added only when it communicates new information.

Before you decide the chart form, filter the information to make your point clear and direct. Add as many layers of information as necessary to convey the key message in each chart, and not one bit more.

Simplify, simplify, simplify!

Answers to ineffective charts on page 15

Use natural increments for the y-axis scale

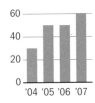

Include a zero baseline in all bar charts

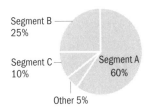

Place the larger segments of a pie chart on the top at 12 o'clock

Understand,
edit and
simplify the
information
and **design**
with your readers
in mind ▌

I am grateful to my professors at the University of Louisville and Yale University who taught me to imagine, to learn, to question and to get to the bottom of things — Alvin Eisenman, Armin Hofmann, Bradbury Thompson, Dorothea Hofmann, Edward Tufte, Inge Druckrey, James Grubola, John Gambell, Mike Kelley, Min Wang, Paul Rand, Phil Wakeman, Steve Skaggs and Ying Kit Chan.

I would like to take this opportunity to thank my colleagues and the professionals I've come to know over the years. You shared with me your ideas and experience and challenged me along the way — Alan Anspaugh, Archie Tse, Bonnie Scranton, Brad Paley, Brian Wu, Charles Blow, Charles Fairweather, Chris McCullough, Christina Rivero, Daniel Beunza, Dave Kansas, David Pybas, Dominic Arbitrio, Dylan McClain, Ellen Lesser Comisar, Floyd Norris, Glenn Kramon, Gordon Akwera, Greg Leeds, Howard Hoffman, Jim Pensiero, Jim Schachter, Joanne Lipman, Joe Dizney, Joe Paschke, John Geddes, Jonathan Pillet, Joseph Tracy, Jovi Juan, Joyce Edwards, Judy Dobrzynski, Karl Gude, Ken Resen, Kevin McKay, Kris Goodfellow, Larry Ingrassia, Laura Chang, Marcus Brauchli, Martin Wattenberg, Matt Murray, Megan Jaegerman, Melinda Beck, Michael Connolly, Nell Cote, Paul Steiger, Rich Meislin, Richard Teitelbaum, Robert Thomson, Roger Black, Sarah Slobin, Seth Feaster, Steve Duenes, Steve Heller, Tom Bodkin, Tomaso Capuano and Tomoeh Tse.

I work with a great group of people at Siegel+Gale who share my passion for simplification — Alan Siegel, Cari Roberts, Charlene Raytek, Christine Mauro, David Srere, Howard Belk, Irene Etzkorn, Lee Rafkin, Madge Dion, Marina Posniak, Mary Quandt, Rachael Keeler, Richard Pasqua, Thomas Mueller and Valentina Miosuro. Thanks to Alan Siegel and Lee Rafkin for their enthusiastic support of this book and to Kate Trogan for a terrific cover design.

For my comrades at WSJinfographics — Andrew Garcia-Phillips, Brett Taylor, Carlos Tovar, Dan Ion, Erik Brynildsen, Francesco Fiondella, Gail Zuniga, Jeff Magness, Jessica Yu, John Won, Josh Ulick, Luis Santiago, Maryanne Murray, Michael Ovaska, Neven Telak, Pat Minczeski, Randy Yeip, Reg Chua, Renee Rigdon, Rich Franconeri, Rubina Madan, Seth Hamblin and Thad Chambers. You were on the front lines with me day in and day out.

My book, your book.

Acknowledgments

My deepest gratitude to my family for their love and encouragement — my husband and best friend Joe Koltisko, my beautiful children Joyce and Michael, 婆婆, 公公, 媽咪, 爸爸, 姨媽, 二舅父, 八舅父, Maggie and Marie. 深感您們的關心和鼓勵, 為我這份努力開心而驕傲。

I am grateful to Edward Tufte, my thesis advisor at Yale, who introduced me to the field of information design. My sincere thanks to Alvin Eisenman who believed in me and was there for me at every turn in the road.

My heartfelt appreciation to many individuals who have helped make this book a success:

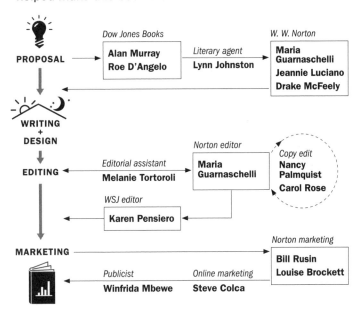

Many other smart professionals at Dow Jones and Norton made this book possible, including but not limited to Paul Kaplan, Anna Oler, Andy Marasia, Ingsu Liu, Eleen Cheung and Nomi Victor.

For my friends — John and Mary Brown, Lisu Chow, Sarah Ling, Angie Yeung, Jim Folino, Grace Sun and Lee Williams — thank you for standing by me and taking my crazy ideas seriously.

Creative Process Revealed

My action wall

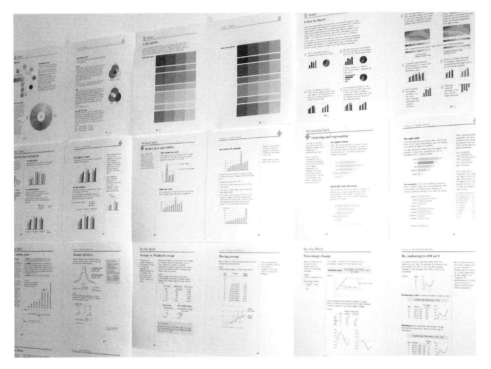

Writing a book distills the writer's creative energy, somewhat like coaxing a genie into a bottle.

When I first decided to pursue this project, I cleared a big wall in my living space. After I had a good number of pages written and designed, I arranged the drafts on the wall in the sequence they appear in the book. Taking the pages outside the book format with a high-impact display brings the creative process to the next level.

Design is an act of expressing and creating. This process helps me to experience the writing and visualization in totality. I can then follow the progression of ideas and visuals and connect all the themes.

This is what brings it all to life.

Index

A

absolute values vs. percentage changes, 107, 126, 128, 129

acronyms, use of, 110

alignment and ordering of numbers, 84–85

alphabetical order, 71, 85

angled or sideways type, 31, 32, 33, 66, 135

area, correct use of, 81

area graphs, 50

arithmetic rate of return, 116–117

assignment chart (work plan), 136

average (mean), 94, 95

average vs. weighted average, 98

B

backward legends, 66

bar charts, 26, 28, 40, 50, 89, 90, 140

   discrete quantities and, 59, 62, 64, 65

   missing data and, 124, 125

   pictograms in, 87, 88

   segmented, 74, 79

   stacked, 74

   see also horizontal bar charts; vertical bar charts

baseline numbers, 27, 106

bell-shaped curves, 96

black ink, "coloring" with, 130–131

black type, for contrast, 45

bold type, 31, 33, 45, 131

broken bars, 68–69

bullet points, 34

C

changes shown with historical perspective, 127

changes vs. absolute values, 107, 126, 128, 129

chart headlines, 32–33

charting, 49–91

   changes vs. absolute values in, 107, 126, 128, 129

   clarity and simplification in, 143

   color use in, see color

   comparable scales in, 60–61, 102–103, 128–129

   context and, 25, 27

   copy style in, 110–111

   direct labeling and, see labeling

   distractions in, 22, 40, 44, 62, 76, 86, 135

   editing and, 20, 28

   essential steps in, 20–21

   estimates and projections in, 26, 63

   historical trends and, 127

   math formulas and facts for, 93–105

   missing or incomplete data and, 124–125

   money matters and, 112–121

   problem-solving and, 123–131

   project planning with graphics, 133–141

   quality vs. quantity in, 28–29

   ranking by attribute or value in, 70, 71

charting (*continued*)
 reference points and, 24, 51
 shading use in, *see* shading
 typography and, 32–33
 of uncorrelated series, 58
 visual impact of, 34–35
 words vs., 22
chart with photo, 35
CMYK (specifying colors), 37
color, 36–47
 bright or muted palettes, 38–39,
  42–43
 for the colorblind, 44–45, 55
 combination pitfalls, 44
 contrast and highlights using black
  ink, 130–131
 describing, 36
 selecting effective, 45
 specifying, 37
 strategic use of, 40–41, 55, 135,
  136, 137, 138
 thematic representation of, 41
 warm and cool, 36
colorblind readers, 44–45, 55
color chart templates, 42–43
color gradient, 46
color palettes, 38–39, 42–43
color scale application, 41, 46–47
comparable scales, 60–61, 102–103,
  128–129
competition tracking, 137
conceptual illustration, 34
condensed type, 31
context, 25, 27

continuous data, 59
contrast and highlights, 44, 45, 130–
  131
copy style in charts, 110–111
cost and resource management, 140–
  141
counting by increments, 52–53, 60, 61,
  89, 103
currencies, 118–121
 charting of, 120–121
 conversion of, 118–119
curves, bell-shaped, 96

D

data:
 continuum of, 34–35
 editing of, 23, 28
 integrity of, 26–27
 richness of, 28–29
 sources of, 20, 23, 26, 69, 124
 verification of, 21
data points:
 in horizontal bar charts, 71
 missing or incomplete, 124–125
 in pictograms, 88, 89
 telling a story with, 29
 in vertical bar charts, 65, 68, 69
decimal numbers, 22, 84, 85, 111
diagrams, 35
direct labeling, *see* labeling
discrete quantity measurement, 62, 64,
  65
display packages, 35
distractions, 22, 40, 44, 62, 76, 86, 135

negative values in, 72
three-dimensional, 22, 62
zero baselines and, 64–65, 126
volatility, mapping of, 46, 95, 99

W

Wall Street Journal, The, 113
weighted averages, 98
whole numbers, 84, 85, 111
work plans, 136

X

x-axis, 51, 66, 110
log scales for, 100

Y

y-axis:
increments for, 52–53, 60, 61, 103
log scales for, 101
scales for, 50, 51, 58–59, 61, 69,
102, 129

Z

zero baselines, 50, 51, 52
horizontal bar charts and, 73
vertical bar charts and, 64–65, 126

About the Author

With over twenty years of experience in information graphics, **Dona Wong** has devoted her career to bridging the analytical and the visual worlds.

Dona became the graphics director for *The Wall Street Journal* in 2001. There she led a team of graphics editors and designers to produce all breaking-news and feature graphics that appeared daily in the newspaper. During her nine-year tenure, she was responsible for setting the graphics standard for the newspaper and affiliates, including wsj.com, *The Wall Street Journal Europe*, and *The Wall Street Journal Asia*. She was instrumental in the redesign of the Money and Investing section in 2002, as part of the paper's overall redesign, which brought full-color graphics to *The Journal* for the first time and received a silver award in the Society of News Design competition.

Dona began her career in visual journalism at *The New York Times* in the 1990s, where she was a graphics editor of the daily Business, Sunday Business, and Monday Media Business sections. Before joining *The New York Times*, Dona developed complex financial graphics for international tax clients at Deloitte & Touche.

Today, Dona is the Strategy Director for Information Design at Siegel+Gale, a global strategic branding firm that is a pioneer in simplifying complex customer communications. Always the consummate designer, Dona's portfolio includes museum publications and posters, brand identity, signage, annual reports, and corporate publications for Fortune 500 companies.

Dona graduated from the University of Louisville, and has an MFA degree from Yale University. She completed her dissertation on information design with thesis advisor Edward Tufte, a recognized authority on data visualization.

She lives in New York City with her husband, Joseph Koltisko, and their two children.

THE WALL STREET JOURNAL.

Every day *The Wall Street Journal* uses information graphics like those detailed in this book to help readers make sense of important news.